GAME ARTIST

THE ULTIMATE CAREER GUIDE

PAUL JONES

Sonola & Jones

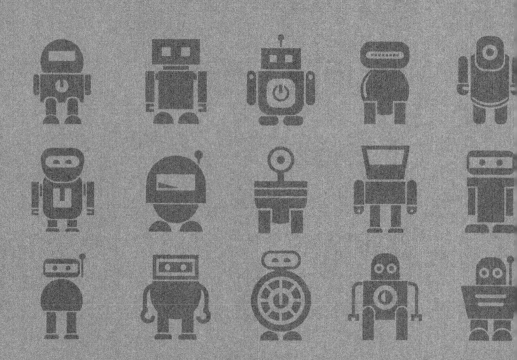

GAME ARTIST

THE ULTIMATE CAREER GUIDE

PAUL JONES

Published by Sonola & Jones Ltd.

Web: www.pauldavidjones.com

ISBN: Book: 978-1-915008-03-9

Publisher: Sonola & Jones Ltd.
Editor: Jasmin Naim
Graphics: Paul Palmer-Edwards and Paul Jones
Chapter illustrations: Paul Jones
Book Layout: Paul Palmer-Edwards
Front cover robots: Shutterstock
Interviewees: Lee Burns, Amber Marie Edwards, Ryan Howard, Jerry O'Flaherty, Luan Vetoreti, Chris Wells and André Wahlgren
Proofreader and Indexer: Cheryl Lenser
Beta Readers: Louise Andrew, Arianne Garin, Rob Lujan, Chris Mielke, Ben Parr, Mickela Sonola and Luan Vetoreti
Website: Jason Harvey and Paul Jones
Special thanks: Luke Davis, Eddie Hilditch, Jeff Morris and Gavin Rothery

Dedicated to everyone who wanted a guiding hand

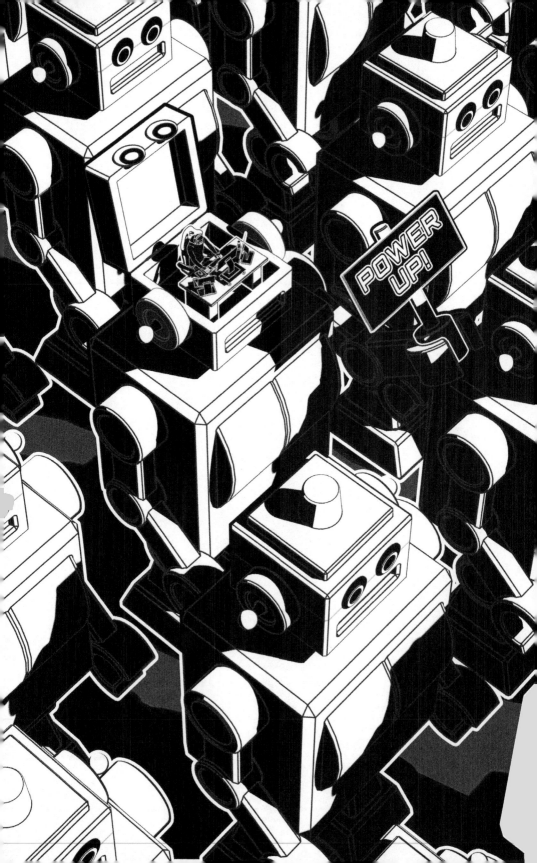

CONTENTS

INTRODUCTION

If I were in your shoes now, and I had my chance again, discovering this book would have been like finding a bar of gold! I'd sit it next to my two other prized books, *Space Wars: worlds and weapons* and *The Making of Judge Dredd* (1995), and I would have read it from cover to cover (instead of just looking at the pretty pictures).

There were times in my career I would have LOVED a guiding hand to make things clear, simple, and less frustrating in this crazy job I've dedicated my life to. I bet you're feeling the same way too and that's why you're reading this book now!

The reality you're facing today is opposite to mine, it's information overload. When you try to find out how to get into the industry, how to get promoted and the real challenges you'll face getting to the top, it's a confusing mix of articles and blog posts; it's nearly impossible to know who's making sense and what their experience is. No amount of searching could have prepared you for the business of making art for video games except by learning the hard way, until now.

I know that it's a risky world out there, but why should it be so hard? Just because everyone has walked the same tightrope until now, why should you? Why not take two steps forward and no steps back? Can you have your cake and eat it? Well, why not?

The fundamental reason for writing this book is to give you the insider's view of working in the games industry, so you start your career with a head packed full of knowledge. If you can't retain it (like me) – don't worry, you can pick this book up at any time and take what you need to keep you moving on up. The goal of this book is simple, you'll find out everything you ever wanted to know about the game artist career path: how to prepare, who to know, where to excel, what your boss reviews you on, getting promotions, financial rewards and bonuses, keeping yourself motivated, avoiding burn-out, everything that you always wanted to know but were unsure who to ask.

I've split the book into five levels, each packed with valuable lessons and insider interviews, delivered in a clear career path timeline, from prospective applicant, to nailing your interview and starting as a Junior Artist, building up skills and being promoted to the roles of Mid, Senior and Principal Artist, and finally into the management roles of Lead Artist and Art Director. Along the way I break each area down further and highlight strategies for success with each role.

I'll let you into a secret now. If you want techniques on improving your art, I suggest you look elsewhere, there are no pixels or polygons to be found here. This book is your opportunity to gain a head start on the competition by reading up on the expectations, hurdles, and ways to navigate game art development. No pen and digital tablet required!

Who is Paul Jones?

I'm a self-taught artist with over twenty-five years of experience, and I've had the opportunity to work on a wide variety of projects for some of the most successful companies, including Epic Games (*Unreal Championship 2* and *Tournament 3*), Rocksteady (*Batman: Arkham City*) and TTFusion (*LEGO City Undercover*). At the time of writing this, I'm an Art Director at Cloud Imperium Games, on the world's largest crowd-funded PC game, *Star Citizen*.

I currently live in Manchester, in the United Kingdom, a city with the honeybee as its logo because, in times gone by, hard work in cotton mills and canals really put this city on the world map. It is where bands like Oasis and the Stone Roses (and so many others, too many to name) struck up and took the world by storm, a place where the world's first computer was built, a place known for celebrating its diverse mix of people and classes, religions and sexuality, all of which I knew nothing about when I first came here, but all of which I now appreciate.

Growing up in a middle-class household, I had it easy in some ways. I lived in a house on an island, to the rear were rolling patchwork hills, and the beach was a ten-minute walk away. Traffic was light and crime was low, except for cow tipping or stealing apples. The Isle of Man is a small rock nestled between the bosom of the UK and the Republic of Ireland, a place known for its Celtic roots and Druid's circle, cats with no tails, black dogs who haunt castles and the world's most dangerous motorcycle road race. My bedroom was only three metres from the road track!

I've mentioned this already, but growing up, I had one art book I loved especially, *Space Wars: worlds and weapons*. It's filled with so many images that were mind-bending both in concept and artistry that, while I had no clue how to replicate it, the sci-fi genre planted a seed that would grow to influence my later life.

Finding tutorials on art and help was hard back in the 1980s. I endured a Paasche airbrush through my teenage years: the masking, the paint spluttering, the noisy compressor; that thing was hard to get good results with and the materials were expensive! By the time I hit sixth form, I had shifted towards the new and emerging subject of Design and Technology (DT). I respected our DT teacher, and he was keen to impart his wisdom and enthusiasm, to help us grow, which was the opposite of how I felt when working for our art teacher.

Life wasn't all straightforward for me, though. At the tender age of nine, I discovered my father had suffered a heart attack at his place of work. He was only 38 and was rushed to hospital. Sadly, he didn't make it, and this defining moment changed my life. I think it's safe to say, it was because of this and my slightly obsessive nature, that I played video games so much as a kid; I loved them and couldn't seem to get enough. Bubble Bobble, Xenon, Speedball, Virus, all of which took me to another reality, one that eventually I made real in a way and has become my career.

The mantra that life is too short has defined my path in the games industry. I specialise in being a generalist because I love the flexibility and opportunities it has provided. Games assets, lighting, rigging, user interfaces, promo art and marketing, I can do whatever a project needs and quickly. Because of that, I've had experiences in many areas of the games industry, which I now get to pass directly onto you.

Your story will be different, the knowledge squeezed into this book is here to help you figure out who you really are, to find your strengths and weaknesses, to question what you want out of your life and your career; I hope you take my experiences and give yourself a head start to define your own journey.

What was my professional journey?

I'm a creative spirited person, I have a need and a drive that demands that I create and if it's not in my day job, it applies to other areas too: artwork, photography, DIY projects, gardening, model car building and painting. At one point I created a real nine-foot long old school chopper!

With that craving, I've followed my passion for working in 3D and on projects that keep me interested and motivated, and I'm always open to a new challenge, whether that's a new country or a crazy project. Here's a quick rap sheet so you can see my greatest hits.

- ❑ I didn't start in games, not even in 3D as a career. Initially I was a kitchen designer and illustrator. I enjoyed it and was one of the fastest, so the sales department were always happy!

- ❑ In the first of a series of pivotal moments, I decided to teach myself 3D and look to buy a PC and software. Weirdly instead though, I got a job (working for free) with the local re-seller of 3DStudio (not Max at that time). Even though I wasn't being paid, I had access to all the hardware and software I needed. Eventually, we were doing paid gigs and creating architectural visualisations for large companies including London's Wembley stadium.

- ❑ After two years I secured a job as a 3D artist for a game called *Soul Master* for a Japanese company called KOEI. I was meant to train in the UK and move to Japan, but sadly it never happened. But it was the start of my longing for adventure.

- I moved back to Manchester and started at a newly formed games company, Warthog Games Ltd. In the four years I was there, we completed *Starlancer* and dabbled in a few other, less popular, titles. By this point I was a Senior Artist and had started a family.

- Guess what? I got itchy feet and moved to London for six months to work on *Dinotopia* for a visual effects company called Framestore. It was a great gig but my wife and I were looking for adventure, so I applied further afield. On being offered a new role, we moved lock, stock and barrel to the USA to work for a new company called Scion which had recently been formed by Epic Games in North Carolina. There I helped to build *Unreal Championship 2* for the Xbox (original). The team was small, but we smashed out a full new game in two years.

- I wasn't looking for a lead role; it found me. I was hungry for things like discipline, folder structures, hitting deadlines and hitting targets (strange I know!) No one else seemed too bothered. It was also odd to me, as I hated making decisions, but I liked structure. By this time Scion had been incorporated into Epic, the tribe went from 25 people to 50 just like that and I was Lead Artist on *Unreal Tournament 3*.

- That three-year period was a wild ride, competing with *Gears of War* for staff and losing core senior people. Some of them I considered my mentors, which led me to start losing sight of what was important. I slowly went into a downward spiral, to the point that I had to step down from my role; I was making too many obstacles to be useful.

- I hired a leadership coach to help me address my communication and confidence issues. Rediscovering your focus can be a double-edged sword, and I knew that if I stayed, I'd continue to be deeply unhappy. I left Epic and wondered for many years whether it was the worst mistake I'd made in my career.

❑ We moved back to the UK where I dropped back into the trenches within the art team again, to make friends and not worry about performance reviews and overachieving while I looked to rebuild my self-confidence. Working on *Batman: Arkham City* proved a pivotal moment, and it felt good to be making artwork again.

❑ London was hard, too hard for me to make a living in, especially with my family to think about and comparatively low wages, so we headed back to our creative roots in Manchester. Opportunity came knocking, and I took on my dream role as Art Director. While working on LEGO games and making the largest LEGO game to date, I could rebuild myself and become a stronger/more authentic and compassionate manager, which was something I'd been striving for.

❑ After two games at TTFusion, the world of sci-fi came calling again. I couldn't resist the pull and moved to work for the third start-up studio of my career, but this time I was building my dream art team. It was part of the network of studios built from the ground up to develop *Star Citizen*. Over time, the company has grown larger and larger, and I currently live and breathe spaceships and space weapons, working daily with a dedicated concept art team.

So, you can see, I've been around the block, as they say. I even had some time training a team in Shanghai, China, as part of working for Epic Games. As a growing artist, I was determined to take opportunities where I could, to not be 'just happy' but to really push myself into unfamiliar territory and experiences. Often, to make the best of your career, you'll need to be prepared to move, not only cities but countries too if you want to work on your favourite games or genres.

None of us have a crystal ball and it's hard to know what direction your career will take, how it'll affect your family or personal life, or what successes and failures you'll experience. Figure 1 shows my journey as a graph; I wanted you to see that, like any pioneer, your confidence will naturally peak and trough. It has to, right? Progression means stepping up to new challenges and taking on the unknown, stepping out of your comfort zone and in essence starting afresh and building those new areas, from the ground up. Sometimes you'll come out on top. Sometimes, you'll take a fall.

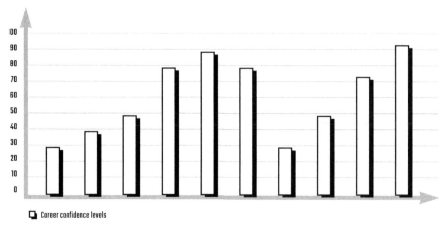

Career confidence levels

Figure 1. I'm thinking this could be a world's first, charting a game artist's personal confidence!!!

With my years and experience in games building, and training teams, I figured now was the time to share, to 'pay it forward'. I wanted to find a way of passing on insider knowledge, so that between us, we can actively make this fledgling industry more transparent, providing clear knowledge of each role, giving the new talent of the industry a leg up by removing some barriers and providing a clear guide to take your career to the next level.

Where do you see yourself in five years' time?

As part of your creative journey, it's important to have a plan. I'll provide you with everything I know, making your guidebook, giving you hints and tips along the way, but for this book to be most effective, I think it's important you have a career plan. I'm convinced you can increase your chances of success by hard work and diligence. And I'm doubly convinced of the phrase 'failure to plan, is planning to fail'.

So, go ahead and ask yourself the simple questions below. Use them to find out a little more about yourself. Do you have a plan or are you just cruising along, hoping to be successful?

- ❏ Where in your career path would you like to be in three to five years?

- ❏ What type of project would you like to be working on?

- ❏ Where in the world would it be?

- ❏ Do you see yourself as a long-term employee?

- ❏ What motivates you to do your best?

- ❏ What skills do you feel you need to improve upon?

- ❏ Do you hit the same roadblock again and again?

In my career, sometimes I knew what I wanted, and grabbed it with both arms and hugged it to death, and sometimes I had no idea, creatively wandering and wondering.

When we made the leap to the USA, we did it almost blindly. It was a true leap of faith. I remember vividly being on the flight to my interview with Scion. I was reading a copy of *The Alchemist* by Paulo Coelho, which was given to me by a friend as a birthday present. It was poignant for me; here I was flying for an interview for a job after following my dream, and reading a book that was mirroring my journey.

In your early career, you'll find it's a simpler time. There's a straightforward ladder to climb. As you read on into this guide, I'll give information on each role, laying the groundwork for more complex and pivotal art roles within the company. I bring the guide; you bring the plan, and together, you'll go further and faster.

How to use this book

Each of the five main sections covers a stage in your career development, including the challenges you'll face and solutions to tackle them. I've packed this book with information, and if you're new to the industry, I recommend you keep this book on your desk or device as a point of reference, dipping in and out of it as you need. Of course, you can read the entire book, and if you're an experienced artist looking to move up to Lead Artist or Art Director then you'll find plenty to think about as you read on.

Level One – Job Applicant

We'll cover the basics here – including how to find your way into the industry and identify what you want, getting a killer portfolio ready for review, understanding what an Art Director is looking for, to finally getting an interview and the ultimate prize of an offer for the role you have been chasing.

Level Two – Junior Artist

This looks at your first few months of working in a games company, what it's like when you start, what are the paperwork and contracts, company benefits, perks and bonuses. We delve into the game development pipeline and typical company hierarchies, so you know who's who. We look at what's expected of you as a recruit and how to succeed and avoid early burn-out, giving you a heads-up on self-care, keeping you productive, having fun and learning to climb the ranks.

Level Three – Mid, Senior and Principal Artist

This is where artists really find their stride and look to advance up the ladder. It's a pivotal period where you decide where you're heading next while mentoring others and working more widely with the development team. I break down how to achieve career progression, and what skills you need for the all-important Personal Development Review (PDR). We cover important areas to upgrade, communication and teamwork, creativity, productivity, self-confidence, mentoring, choosing to specialise (or not) and when you feel it's time for a change, how best to make an exit strategy.

Level Four – Lead Artist

We explore the transition from working purely with artwork to having managerial responsibilities. We look at management techniques, understanding both yourself and your team, how to develop and drive a successful team, dealing with tricky situations, meetings, presentations, staff reviews and negotiation. Plus, a section dedicated to you and how to set time aside for thinking, planning, and maybe even some artwork.

Level Five – Art Director

This section covers positioning yourself for the high-stakes role of Art Director. What to expect when you work with executives and publishers, team deadlines, leading from the front, managing your team and the creative process. We examine working with internal and external teams, concept artists and game team artists, outsource studios and how to get the best from them and how it all comes together to make a game.

 Like your favourite buffet, you don't have to pack it all in at one sitting, you can come back to it again and again and pick away at the sections that concern you the most.

So where do we start? That's simple, like any game; at Level One!

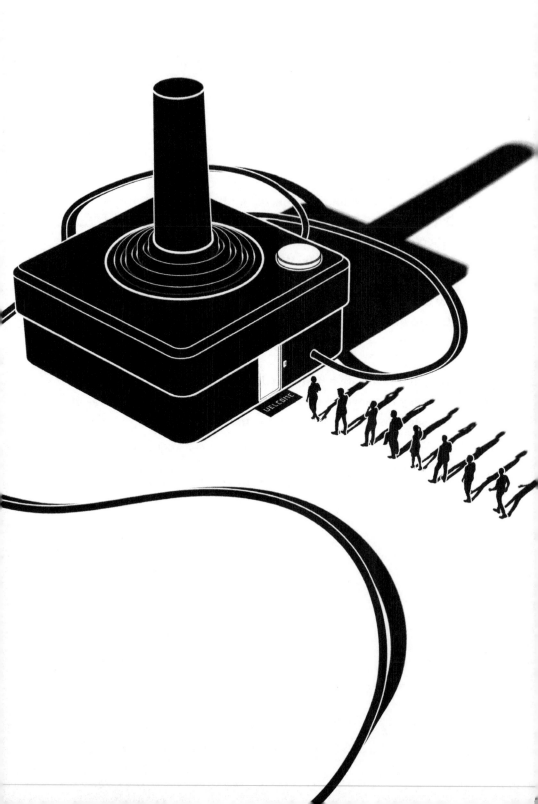

LEVEL
01

JOB APPLICANT

GETTING YOUR FOOT IN THE DOOR

I knew someone who dressed in a full Star Wars stormtrooper suit to drop off their resume. The tactic was effective, as it certainly got them noticed, but it was their strong portfolio of work that got their foot in the door. There are more straightforward methods to get into the Games Industry that don't require real-world model making skills!

Your artwork represents you, and good artwork is the key that unlocks interview doors. After that, it's a straight-up personality test, but let's not rush ahead just yet. If you want to work on world-class game titles, the work begins way before you even send out your resume.

The job market is getting more competitive year on year, with applicants battling for coveted roles in the major studios. Your journey into becoming a Game Artist starts with creating a killer portfolio; art is everything, well almost. We will delve into the murky world of the job interview, covering various processes to give you an insight into how to put your best foot forward and the common pitfalls to avoid.

By the end of this chapter, you'll have a clear idea of the preparation and thought you'll need to put into presenting your work and giving yourself a higher chance of breaking into the Games Industry and being one step closer to your dream career.

1.1 CONTENT PREPARATION

1.2 THE INTERVIEW

LEVEL
1.1

CONTENT
PREPARATION

WHAT ART DIRECTORS LOOK FOR IN YOUR PORTFOLIO

Your portfolio is the holy grail for applying for a job. This may sound a little like the premise for an action-adventure movie, but it's true! Ignore everything else (initially). This is where you win or lose, the place where everything you do matters, and the first impression is always the strongest.

It sounds dramatic, I know. As an Art Director (AD) and a hiring manager, I ignore everything else in the job application and go straight to the pretty pictures, and it's always refreshing to see a strong portfolio from a wannabe junior. Ultimately, I want to be impressed. I won't be measuring you against a Senior Artist; with a good portfolio as a junior you'll have a higher chance of getting your foot in the door, my expectations are lower but you still need to show me want I want to see.

So, now you may be thinking, 'What does he want to see, what if I don't show it, how can I read his mind?' You can't! And you don't need to. It's less about the type of content, more about the process you are showing, your development and your attention to quality.

Let's quit the guessing game. It's probably most helpful if I just tell you what I look for in a portfolio. I've hired a lot of artists in my time and looked at countless applications, so, let's get to it!

A good first impression

Lead with your best artwork first. This isn't new advice but it's true and people still ignore it. Don't include the piece that took you 100 hours to make, but still turned out slightly crappy. As a busy AD, I'll look at the image and make a judgement, and it won't be good. That's why it is always good to have a peer group who'll review your work and support you in pushing out your best artwork. That's what I want to see – high quality content.

Creativity and technical ability

When you're early in the learning process, most of your effort is focused on problem solving and the technical process of taking an idea all the way through the art pipeline (modelling, UV mapping, shaders, and animation) to the final finished asset. Only once you've become familiar with the process will it be easier to conjure up more original creations. In the past, the juniors I hired showed strong technical prowess and strong visuals, the scene or object was well executed and presented, and showed a determination to create something fresh.

The spark

Call it what you like; spark, secret sauce, it's the thing that makes me say, 'Oh, that's cool'. If I were to put this into words, I guess it would build upon the creativity and technical ability section. It's the knowledge that you're a would-be junior and you've created something that's well delivered, thought out and shows unexpected artistic maturity.

Cleanliness

It doesn't matter what sub-section of game art you are talking about, it could be sketches, modelling, texturing, shaders, lighting, cameras, or animations; you can be clean and efficient or you can be dirty and messy and achieve a similar result. Clean and efficient is the preferred option if you are unsure! Often I request additional supporting images to see examples of UV layouts, shader networks, wireframes for polygon topology, so yes, tidy is good.

Artistic journey

If I can see evidence of your artistic journey, that's great. Polished images are part of the final process, but it's also about the journey. I like to see the path you took, and how your work has improved as you've spent time crafting your skills.

Clear descriptions

I find descriptions of a candidate's portfolio pieces are often vague or rambling. Keep descriptions of the work clear and simple. Let your work do most of the talking but give context, and above all else give credit if some work belongs to someone else, for example, a collaborative project.

Easy to find website and links

While your work should do the talking, if I can't find the images easily, your portfolio review isn't going to go well. I do normally chase things down; I can't help it, but there's a part of me that wants to say tough luck and put the application in the rejected pile. I know you've made the effort to apply, so what's another ten seconds for searching? But some ADs won't bother.

Easy to read resume

A simple and elegant resume is best. Graphs that tell me how proficient you are in Photoshop look pretty, but what do they mean? Everyone's metric is different. I want to be able to find out who you are, quickly and easily. I get applications that come with no portfolio; by that I don't mean missing links, I mean, no artwork! If you're missing a portfolio, then don't waste your time applying. No artwork, then no chance, regardless of 'I love playing games'.

PORTFOLIO PROCESS

Portfolios are the curation of your own art show. You're the star and it's worth spending the time and going the extra mile to curate the strongest portfolio you can. You'll only have a slender opportunity to present to your prospective new employer, so make every second of their time count to boost your chances of success.

Regardless of your career path, bedroom Wacom warrior, freelancer, indie or AAA game artist, good artwork is good artwork. It's universal and the person reviewing your portfolio will be able to uncover what they're looking for.

So, you've put together your best work, but what specifically will help your work stand out?

Presentation

Clear and consistent presentation is key. How you deliver your visuals influences whether you're a success or go down in flames. Your portfolio should be clear and professional, with no memes, no NSFW scribbles dotted about, just excellent imagery with clear explanations.

If you've been working as part of a team, call out what you did and give credit to the other team members. In the games industry, it's rare to fully own something. It gives a great impression if you have the strength of character to give kudos to your co-workers. If you've referenced a concept artist's artwork for inspiration, make sure you give a shout-out, there are no prizes for pretending it was all your own idea.

Subject

The role you are applying for and your level of experience will dictate what you show as part of the portfolio. For example, a prop, weapon, or character artist will often show a single asset. It might be a space crate, rocket launcher, or a shopkeeper, for example.

If you're applying for the role of environment artist, then your scene can be more complex and include more assets; and often include additional work explaining the modular asset set used to create the scene or highlighting a particular hero asset.

When you're working in collaboration with artists, make sure that your work is clearly identified as yours, and which belongs to other artists, and credit them accordingly.

Lighting

In short, lighting makes or breaks your work. Good lighting can make an average asset look good on first impression, and a great asset can look next level. The key is having quality assets to work with, and the lighting further accentuates the visuals. The opposite can also be true, and many a great asset has been let down by poor lighting.

So, it really pays to spend some time on figuring out what presents your work best to the viewer. Artists sometimes shy away from this, but with practice and an understanding of what you are trying to achieve, good lighting will ensure your work shines above the rest.

Composition and cameras

Every scene tells a story. You want to figure out what you're trying to tell the viewer. Let's break this down into some simple examples and what composition is required for each.

1. Single asset showcase (a prop, weapon, vehicle, character, etc). The focus is the asset. Your scene should be uncluttered and well lit. You might have some turntables set up to rotate your camera or the object, with a few additional camera angles to highlight detail or materials you're proud of.

2. Asset as part of a collection. The focus is the scene, not the individual asset. Let's say you have built an environment, some ruins nestled within a green valley, a cart and horse wander along a track, in search of the glowing staff of eternity. Now it's about storytelling, how you arrange your assets, how you light the scene, where you position the camera, what type of weather or mood, and what lens you use all impact on the image/movie.

To help define your narrative, consider these elements to understand what makes an arresting piece of work (we'll use the previous cart/castle as the example):

- The subject (Is it the cart or the castle? Lighting and depth of field can help separate items.)

- The relationship of the subject to the camera (Up close is more intimate, far away is more distant.)

- The camera lenses and aspect ratio (50mm lens are good for single assets, wide for when you need to squeeze that little bit more into the shot, long lenses for when you want to compress the scene and make the castle look close to the cart/rider when they still have a long way to travel.)

- ❏ The lighting direction (Often foreground objects are darker. Once you notice it, you see it everywhere! Lighting directs the eye, often you'll see a castle bathed in sunlight, surrounded by dark clouds, the cart/rider will have a small lamp light which helps attract your attention.)

- ❏ The type of lighting (Full sunlight, dappled, overcast or lightning conditions plus the direction and elevation of your light enhance the story.)

- ❏ The shadows (Soft and disperse in a foggy swamp or strong and direct from the sun or an alien energy source? Either helps to convey emotion.)

- ❏ Atmospherics (Cloudy, low-lying mist, distant atmospherics add depth and subtle colour to the scene.)

- ❏ The colour tones (Is your scene mainly muted colours with bright wildflowers? Vibrant greens and golden sun, dark and ominous greys and blues with hints of warm light only from the lamp?)

- ❏ Contrast (High or low contrast?)

- ❏ Palette (Contrasting or complementary?)

You can apply this to other work you find on the internet, slowly you'll start seeing common techniques used among the art community to feed into your own work.

Thought process

If, for example, you have designed and built a weapon or space crate, you probably think it's the best thing out there, but the viewer might not know why, unless you show them, so make clear how it works. Support it with an animation, or a cutaway showing the workings, show it in isolation and in situ if possible.

Show your workings out and sketches so people can see clearly how you arrived at your destination and the decisions you made to get there. Show your texturing skills or material node network if it's complex, clever, or out of the ordinary.

Often artists have multiple silos of work, their main portfolio site with their best work on ArtStation or their website, a blog section that has some behind the scenes and workings out and a social media page that covers personal interests. It's a three-pronged attack, showing your artwork, your process and your personality.

Extra-curricular endeavours

It's great to be able to show your other hobbies like photography, model making, painting, rock climbing, drumming, travel, etc. I'm sure you can fill in the blanks. This reveals more than a digital make-believe world, that you can appreciate the real things around you and push yourself in other ways. There is no CTRL-Z in real life, and you have to work hard to get quality results. From a hiring manager's point of view, it shows more of your personality and tenacity prior to the interview.

> *You never know what can tip the scales and show your interviewer that spark that persuades them to give you a chance. I interviewed at Framestore CFC and had a strong digital portfolio with a variety of game subjects and styles; however, it wasn't until Alec Knox started looking through my photography section that the interview pulled away from the edge of a cliff, showing him a greater understanding of artistic principles, composition and lighting. I got the job as a TD (technical director – lighting artist) and went to work on Dinotopia.*

Show artwork that matches your target company

Showcasing artwork where the subject and style are opposite to the work your target company produces will get you rejected straight away. For example, if you draw cute kittens by hand but the project you are applying to makes hardcore sci-fi 3D art you will not match. Or if you work in a kitchen at the local cafe and have always wanted to work in games but you have no experience and no portfolio (yes, this happens more often than you would think), you are wasting time and effort again, so start learning the software and gain some experience.

Healthy life, healthy work

We've all done it; kicked back after a hard day, had a beer or a glass of wine and worked steadily away into the small hours, thinking the work being produced is super amazing. Waking up to a new day, you'll see with horror the work you've created. Alcohol and tiredness affect your judgement in everything you do, so be selective about what you put in your portfolio.

> *I once worked with an artist, who was super talented but still early in their career. In the evening they would spend time honing their craft, building 3D, smashing out renders while enjoying a few beers. It became a regular thing and in the small hours they would email their results. The next day, we'd come into work and open our mail to see the creative, slightly drunken endeavours. Often the enthusiasm was amazing but in reality, the images weren't as good as the hype.*

If you're going to seriously work, don't get drunk and give your work the time to breathe. You need time to reflect on what you've done, to see if there's anything that can be improved before you send it on. It's worth the delayed gratification!

Be critical (but be kind to yourself)

It's crucial to be critical with your work and it's better to show one or two images of something that's great rather than eight of something average or unfinished. It's the hardest thing to be critical of your own work, so I recommend teaming up with someone who can be helpful yet critical, and vice versa, so that between the two of you, you level each other up.

WHERE TO SHOW YOUR ARTWORK

Think of this as your shop front, showcasing you and your artwork. That's why it's important to choose the right place to host your portfolio. For those reviewing your creations (Lead Artist/Art Directors/Recruiters), it's vital they can access the information quickly and easily.

If your website has problems with speed, connectivity or page navigation, your application could fail regardless of the quality of work. In my mind there are two strong avenues to pursue and each has its own merits; there is no right answer, just preference.

Portfolio websites – The current premier place for artists to show their work is www.ArtStation.com. It's clean and simple and presents your work with zero fuss. Others use Squarespace or similar managed sites and ultimately it depends on your budget, but even if you're on a free site, think about these things when you set it up.

- Alongside your portfolio, make sure to also include a professional image of yourself, add a custom banner, and describe yourself. You're the product, so sell yourself, not just your work.

- It's recommended you provide additional images of your subject, different angles, lighting or situation. It definitely improves the viewing experience.

- Images that are work in progress (WIP) can be added to the blog section but be sure to provide a description about the work and what you were trying to achieve. Inform the reader and take them on a journey, that keeps them more engaged.

Dedicated hosted website – Developing your own website can pose a higher risk than a dedicated portfolio platform unless you are technically savvy. The benefits are that you own the domain and can make your site into whatever you want. If you do buy your own domain and host, I would recommend the following:

❑ Make sure you have all your pages sanity checked by a friend.

❑ Confirm the website address works as expected.

❑ Check all the pages load without errors.

❑ Confirm the site works across all formats, including PC and mobile.

❑ Review all the content to ensure you have credited any work that isn't completely yours to the rightful owner(s).

❑ Examine all the text content for grammar and spelling.

❑ Review your pages to ensure the website flows, does it make sense when you navigate it?

❑ Check your images and pages load fast enough, because some providers have slow servers.

Social Media – Isn't the place to host your portfolio, however, it's a great way for people to get involved with you and your process and easy to signpost viewers back to your portfolio site.

 In your application, your links must work! Most busy managers won't have the time to hunt around to find your portfolio via another means. They will reject your application.

RESUME READY

Your resume comes a close second in the race to create the perfect application. It complements what your portfolio shows by telling the story, and is where your previous hard work is boiled down to its most potent and basic form.

From your resume, your prospective employer can quickly find where you have worked, on what projects, your length of service and level of seniority. A well-executed resume isn't just banged out, it's treated with the same care as your portfolio, given the same level of scrutiny and peer review, so keep these things in mind when you craft yours. Above all, use a spelling and grammar check!

What to include

- Keep your information condensed, ideally to fit on one page, or two at a maximum.

- Use a Word template or a web-based resume builder to save time and effort.

- Choose a template that represents you, professional with clean fonts and modern layout.

- Split your resume into clear sections: Name and contacts, Personal profile, Work history, Academic background, Achievements, Skills and interests.

- Your profile section should summarise you and what you provide as a professional.

- Skills and interests are important to give the reader a hint of who you are besides just an artist. If you don't have any, maybe now it's time you got some!

What to avoid

- Avoid crazy fonts or bold colours even if the game you are applying for has that comic look. Remain professional and let your portfolio do the talking.

- Delete charts that say you are 80% proficient in types of software, it means nothing to anyone but you.

- ❏ Don't embellish your resume with skills you don't have or work you didn't do, it's a high-risk strategy and not a good way to start your new job.

- ❏ Say no to silly email addresses, such as bigbadartist99@live.com. Get a new one, ideally your name.

- ❏ No need for date of birth, religion, or gender, it's all about you as an artist.

 Remember, you are crafting your own brand, everything counts towards you presenting a unified experience, something that will give the reviewer every reason to take your application to the next stage.

COVER LETTER

Done right, a cover letter can give some high-level insights into who you are as a person and can really elevate your application.

What to include

- ❏ Include your details, the date, address, portfolio link, email address and telephone number.

- ❏ Keep the main body of your letter concise, introducing yourself and stating which role you are applying for.

- ❏ Use a maximum of three paragraphs to explain your high-level skills, picking out some interesting points about you and your work. What separates you from the crowd?

- Tailor your letter to the company you are applying to, make a link between you/your work/your desire to work for company X.

- To finish, include a quick line expressing your eagerness to be contacted and sign off with 'Sincerely' and your name.

What to avoid

- Don't write sentences like this: 'I've played video games all my life and have a deep desire to work in the games industry'. Yes, we've all played lots of games, that's taken for granted.

- Don't say it's been a long-time dream to work in the industry but then not supply any artwork or provide a link to your portfolio. The number of applications that come through with this delusion would surprise you.

- Don't be clever and say, 'I'm sure you agree, my work is awesome. I look forward to your call'. It never works, and your ego has already killed your opportunity.

- Don't send your application to all the open positions a company offers on their website. Blind firing is a poor tactic, as the hiring software we use highlights candidates who have done this, and it ultimately suggests that you don't know where your strengths lie. Could it be that you don't have a strength at all? If that's the case, regroup and start working on an asset that you love to build, focus and the rest will follow.

 Feel that you're an artist and not a writer? Don't worry, you can make use of a cover letter template to build yours out. Follow up with Grammarly.com or Prowritingaid.com to show where you can improve your word craft.

USING A RECRUITMENT AGENCY

In the past recruiters have worked well for me because they often provide access to roles that would otherwise be unknown, or at least you might get to them first before they become common knowledge (though this isn't always the case). Most of my top jobs came from using their services, including Framestore, Scion Studios/Epic Games and Rocksteady in London.

What can they do for you?

❑ Recruiters provide you with opportunities.

❑ Roles can sometimes be hot off the press and not even on the internet.

❑ Their service goes two ways. They:
  ❑ do the legwork and match you to suitable roles.
  ❑ sell you to prospective employers, working out favourable deals and helping you get the best outcome.

❑ An agency will help with negotiations over salary and benefits, which is an added bonus if you dread face-to-face discussions or don't feel confident in tackling them.

Does it cost you anything?

In short, no. It costs you nothing, which is great, and there's nothing stopping you from using multiple recruiters. But if you aren't paying, then who is?

Game developers use recruiters to do a lot of the initial searching for candidates, for the more sought-after roles, or for those troublesome roles which the company has yet to fill. If the game developer hires you via a recruiter, the game developer pays a fee. If you leave before completing a year, your employer won't be pleased, so it's important you aim to take the right job and a good recruiter can help you make that decision.

WHAT DOES IT LOOK LIKE FROM THE RECRUITER'S POINT OF VIEW?

I've worked with Lee Burns, a seasoned recruiter based in the UK, who's been finding talented artists roles for many years. I asked him some probing questions about his day-to-day operations and invited his thoughts on the overall recruitment process to give you an insight into the other side of the process.

Q. Who are you, how long have you been doing it, and what motivates you to keep doing it?

A. My name is Lee and I've worked as a recruiter for over 15 years, with 9 plus of those spent recruiting for the video games industry. I suppose my prime motivator for doing what I do is my general love of the industry, both on a personal and professional level. It's such a vibrant and creative pool of people that we deal with daily and being able to chat to people about their passions, interests and games and call that work is a real pleasure.

In terms of why recruitment, I think it is the opportunity to talk and network with people at all levels of the industry and then use those relationships to help people secure their dream job and next career move. Oddly, in my mind, it is kind of like a jigsaw puzzle. I spend my time looking for that rightly shaped piece that will fit and finish off the picture. It's hugely satisfying when you present a job offer to a candidate who has worked so hard to land that dream role... it can be a little emotional. :)

Q. Why do you think people should use a recruiter?

A. I don't... or at least I don't think they should use a recruiter all the time. A good recruiter can save a manager a lot of time and energy when they are looking to hire for a specific set of skills or a particular niche / specialised role. They will go out to the market and proactively attract good candidates to your business, not just wait for people to apply. That I think is the real value.

I spend a lot of my time understanding what good candidates are looking for and then presenting the right opportunities in the right way to get them interested in talking to potential employers. Good people are rarely actively looking or applying to roles, but they are usually willing to listen, especially if the recruiter has done their job right and built up some trust and credibility.

Q. What are the top three most common mistakes that an applicant will make?

A. 1. Not preparing or preparing the wrong way

When moving through to interview stages, a candidate should try to get an understanding of what type / style of interview they are going into. Will it be technical, conversational, etc? Usually the first-stage interview will be classed as a casual chat / conversation which is fine, but it is important to still do some homework.

If the studio has a recent game they have released, try to play it, or at least watch videos if you can't. Re-read the job spec and make sure you know how your experience relates to each bullet point. If the job spec says, "must have experience of Maya", then be ready to answer the question "Tell me about your experience with Maya".

2. Getting overly creative on their CV (resume)

There is plenty of conflicting advice out there about what you should and shouldn't put in a CV. CVs are subjective to the person reading them; what one hirer will love, another will hate, so there is no perfect CV layout. Having said that, in my opinion there are some things worth considering and getting overly creative and flashy with your CV is one of them. Yes, you want it to stand out, yes you want to be noticed of course, but you can't let that get in the way of having a CV that is easy to read and understand. If you are applying to a creative role, a little bit of flair is fine, but let your portfolio do most of the talking. That's where you show off your artistic / design talent.

3. Personal work

For juniors especially, you should always try to show personal work where possible, if it is of a decent standard. At a junior level for most disciplines an employer is looking to hire talent but also natural passion and drive. A manager can teach you to be a better artist / designer or how to use a specific engine or tool, but they can't teach you to want to learn or be passionate about your job.

Personal work shows that passion and desire to improve in your chosen discipline. Your uni work is great, but someone made you do that. The work you did during your internship or that 6-month placement you did is good but, again, you did that because someone made you do it. Where is the work you did because you enjoy character art or level design or whatever your discipline is? Show that little Unreal Engine level you made because you wanted to have a play around with the new engine update. Or that character model you made because you wanted to have an experiment with something more fantasy and cartoony to improve your skills.

Q. What value does a recruiter provide?

A. A good recruiter can / should be adding value in all sorts of ways. They will save the studio time and money by acting as an initial filter of candidates so that the hiring managers are not getting swamped with non-relevant profiles. They expand a studio's reach by proactively going out and attracting candidates to a studio that would most likely have not been aware or interested in the first place.

Personally, I think the biggest value a really good recruiter provides is the relationship they build with a candidate. The main part of my job is taking the time to understand what motivates a person, what do they like about their current position, what would they change, what do they want to do with their career, where do they want to work, what types of projects are they most interested in? I can use that information to present the right opportunities to that candidate and relay those key motivators to a client where appropriate.

Q. From your point of view, what makes a candidate stand out from the rest? The one that you know is a winner?

A. It's never an exact science knowing who will be a hire, as so much can come down to personal preference on the side of the hiring manager. However, a candidate that takes the time to tailor their application to a role, spends time keeping their portfolio up to date and is able to articulate their experience, passions and interests tends to do well.

Q. Can a candidate use more than one recruiter at a time?

A. Yes, but try to focus on spending your time with the recruiters you feel you have the best relationship with. Do they listen to you, are they easy to get hold of, do they phone you back quickly, do they come to you with relevant and interesting opportunities? I would personally avoid any recruiters where they make you feel you are just another candidate.

The one thing to absolutely do is control very carefully where your information goes. Make it clear to any recruiter that you don't want your information (CV) being submitted to any company without your permission first. They should not be doing that anyway, but if you find out they have, then I would ditch them at the first opportunity.

Q. As a recruiter, what's the most frustrating part of working with candidates and how can that frustration be avoided, are there simple things to be done/learnt?

A. Recruiting can be amazingly rewarding and frustrating in equal measure, really, for all sorts of reasons. At the end of the day we are dealing with people on both sides of the process, so anything can happen. I think you very quickly learn to not sweat the small things in recruitment or you would lose your mind.

Good and honest communication on both sides, though, I think is the easiest thing to do to avoid frustration. Don't feel you need to tell the recruiter what they want to hear, "Yes I really do love that company I interviewed with honest". If you didn't like them, you should feel comfortable enough with your recruiter to say, "You know what, I think they are a bit rubbish and here is why".

ART TESTS AND WHAT TO EXPECT

Why do companies have art tests?

For any advertised role, a company can receive hundreds of applications, all vying for that top spot. As a hiring manager, when an application contains all the right stuff, life is simple. The quality, the content, and the experience is all in the application, but this is far from the norm.

I'd estimate that half of the applications received show promise. They show a hint of creative spark. I've mentioned this before, it's a recurring theme. The right candidate, given the right conditions, can become an exceptional artist for the company, with mentoring and a positive environment. Though their portfolio is lacking, they have the skills to be great one day.

But promise alone isn't enough to make me want to call the candidate for an interview. I need evidence. That's why the art test exists. We know you want the job, you applied, so are you willing to go the extra mile to commit to an art test?

Sometimes, especially for companies with high expectations, the art test can be quite tough, taking up to 30 hours to complete. It comprises not only the fundamentals of modelling and texturing, but also modularity, lighting, mood, colour and composition skills. Understandably, it's not for everyone and for some, it can help to focus their thinking. 'Do I really want to work for this company, am I prepared to commit?'

What's the process? – Normally you're given an asset to build in a certain amount of time, sometimes using specific software. You'll be expected to interpret the written direction or concept art and deliver a game ready asset to the best of your skill level in a style expected by the company.

Before you start – Way before you twitch the mouse and dive headfirst into the test, make one hundred percent sure you are clear on what is being asked of you. How long is the test? What's the expected delivery method? It's ok to ask the company for clarification and also to delay a test if you face some trouble (moving house, or a family emergency, etc).

Good communication is key at this initial stage, and poor communication won't go unnoticed.

Time management – They may ask you to provide evidence of how long your test took. If you spent 50 hours instead of 30, then it indicates some issues. A good interviewer will discuss timing with you to pinpoint the pivotal factors. The time you allocated to the various parts of the test shows your relative experience and how well you manage your process.

On completion – Double check the delivery requirements, then submit your completed test. Now it's a waiting game. If you've heard nothing after a week or two, it's perfectly acceptable to inquire if the company has reviewed your work. Not everyone works the same, some may ask you not to contact them, some may be more welcoming.

The results – If you are successful, the agency or HR department will contact you to arrange an interview. Congratulations, you have reached the next stage! But if you don't make the grade, ask for feedback on your test if the company is willing to find out what went well/badly and where you could improve next time.

As mentioned, completing this art test shouldn't be taken lightly. It's an achievement in its own right, regardless of the result, the chances are you've juggled multiple lives/jobs and dedicated serious hours and brain space to get it done by the agreed deadline.

Successful or not, recognise your own achievement, take time to evaluate and reflect on what went well and what could have gone better. This is great practice, and you'll find a similar process when you are working for a games company. It's all about taking the critique and eventually moving on up.

 Keep persisting, keep seeking answers on areas that are unclear, keep crafting, and that interview will happen one day.

LEVEL
1.2

THE INTERVIEW

RESEARCH LIKE A BOSS

This stage is all about the research. You're going into an unknown environment with unknown interviewers, do you suffer from sweaty palms and cotton mouth (dry mouth), do you lose your train of thought or talk incessantly? An interview can cause a fight-or-flight response, especially when you really have your heart set on the job. So how do you overcome these hurdles to help you in your hour of need?

Fear or anxiety is apprehension about the unknown, it's projecting what might happen. The problem is, you just don't know. I don't think you can control everything, but I've found the task of research helps to reduce that unknown quantity. So, do some digging, see who or what comes up in your search. Even if it doesn't have all the answers, it can help you develop some good questions for your interviewer.

As a starting point, I recommend you look at these areas:
- Company history
- Previous games
- Studio boss
- Interviewer(s)
- Previous employees
- Culture
- Salary and benefits

Many of these are a sub-set of something larger. Use the places listed below to find what you need, activate your inner super sleuth, and see what you can uncover, you might be (pleasantly) surprised!

Companies House (UK) – The Companies House website is useful for finding details of company directors and yearly financial results, nuggets of information about titles, annual turnover, number of staff and bonuses. There may also be links to parent companies if they are multinational, which can give you further insight.

LinkedIn – A well-known global site for professionals. It's the place to go for making connections and finding people, as well as searching their career backgrounds. Recently LinkedIn has become more of a one-stop shop with people posting articles and self-promotion. I would be careful of recommendations though, have you noticed they are always positive? Think about it, you don't ask your nemesis to post a review of you, do you?

Glassdoor – A website dedicated to giving an insight into how a company operates, comprising happy and sad employees. I've read comments about some of my previous employers and they are interesting, but ask yourself how much you think is true. Do the comments make sense or is the reviewer a rotten apple? Note the dates when comments were posted to see if you can find any trends; is the company getting better where it initially had failings? Are you ok with some of those failings? As a newcomer to the industry, it's hard to know what's acceptable, but culture comments or harsh crunch conditions are a real red flag.

Google – Google will show you which games the company has released. It also lists who worked on what. From this list you can look up the Lead or the Art Director and do more digging into who the personalities are at the head of the project.

Social media and YouTube – Keep on sleuthing! Use social media and YouTube to continue to build your dossier, so that you go to your interview fully prepped and ready.

Salary sites – I've left the best to last, maybe because salary is the hardest thing to research. Countries, regions and departments all pay differently. Artists appear to get paid more in the USA, but the cost of living can be high in certain cities, so effectively you won't be much better off. These are some sites where you can find out more about pay and see what the going rate is for someone with your experience:
- www.GamesIndustry.biz
- www.loveforgames.com/salary/
- www.Skillsearch.com

You won't be tested on this digging; it's really an opportunity for you to find out more about the company and the culture. All along the interview process, you'll be gathering information from your interviewers, the company, and their culture.

Ready and prepped? Now it's interview time.

THE INTERVIEW PROCESS

By now you've done the hard work of the writing, emailing, portfolio and the art test, so now it's the personality test. Are you who you say you are? Do you have the skills you say you have? Do you present as modest, a hard head, a rascal, or a charlatan? Those are the sort of things your interviewer will want to know.

> *My most extensive interview was at Epic Games; it was also one of my best. They flew me to North Carolina in the USA on a whirlwind trip. This journey had started long before the flight though, a month before with a long-awaited phone call.*
>
> *I had thought that I'd blown the interview and needed to look elsewhere. Not having heard anything for weeks, I naturally imagined that I'd done or said something wrong that had put me out of the running.*
>
> *The position was for a Senior Artist but my major downside was that I had no Unreal Engine experience and this opportunity was to make Unreal Championship 2 in Unreal Engine 2 on the Xbox.*
>
> *To cut a long story short, my interview included these small social tests too:*
>
> ❑ *A drop-in visit from Epic's then Lead Game Designer, Cliff Bleszinski.*
>
> ❑ *A BBQ at Co-founder, Mark Rein's house that evening.*

> *Talking to many of the stalwart staff, people that already had large reputations within the community (no pressure!) and further conversations the following day.*
>
> *They eventually offered me the job. I worked from home while they completed the visa and paperwork, and we sold our house and left friends and family. Within six months we had moved with my two kids and I was on site, full time in Cary, USA.*

With games recruitment being a global process, candidates are just as likely to be in a different part of the world. Companies have adapted to make the most of the hiring market, and a popular process is the two-stage interview. Large companies with deep pockets have the resources to fly you over for your second-stage interview, although normally senior roles get the special treatment.

Online

Whether you use Skype, Zoom, Teams or one of the many other options, the list is growing regarding which software to use, but the pre-checklist stays the same.

- Ahead of time, check that your camera and microphone are working. Test them on a friend to make sure the day before.

- Check your desktop. Make sure your background image won't cause offence and that you have no strange files visible if you are going to share screens.

- Check your surroundings. Is there anything behind you that will distract?

- Become familiar with using the software ahead of time, sharing screens and work is not uncommon.

- If you are encountering technical difficulties/glitches, you can resort to your phone and ear buds.

- Let your interviewer and company know ahead of time if you can't connect for any reason, and as a last resort, you can ask to reschedule.

- Prepare by looking over your art test because they will ask you about your results and if you would change anything in hindsight.

- Have a glass of water on standby.

- Enjoy! You are talking about you and your work; you got this!

On site

Interviews in person give you a great opportunity to experience the vibe of the office; how busy is it, what's the seating layout, do people seem happy, what's the decor and lighting, do they have any goodies like commissary, gym or basketball court and car parking? Obviously this is subject to our post-COVID world, however, working face-to-face is likely to return in some form.

Pre-interview

- Be presentable. Yes, I know game devs are a mixed bag and that they dress how they like, but save some of that for when you have the job! At least turn up clean and refreshed looking.

- Write down your questions. If you get nervous and forget them, you have them right in front of you to read.

- Check your details. Do you have the right address; do you have the correct studio? It's a simple mistake to make, but potentially fatal.

- Plan your route. When you ask Google to tell you the travel time, make sure you enter the time you intend to travel, so it gives you an accurate prediction. Traffic will ebb and flow depending on the day.

- Have a printed copy of the important details, including address, which entrance, the interviewer's name and phone number.

- Take some water, just in case. Your travel time may be long, and the studio may not offer refreshments. Not all interviewers are well versed in looking after interviewees.

- Aim to arrive early. You want to feel prepared and not flustered. There could be documents to sign (eg Non-Disclosure Agreements) and you may need a quick trip to the bathroom.

- Stuck in traffic or some situation that's making you late? Contact the studio and let them know; hopefully they will push your interview to a later slot.

- More senior roles will involve a lunch with devs to chat about you and your career and skills. It's all part of finding out how rounded you are as a person and an artist.

 I travel with a small bag of goodies, such as a high energy snack bar just in case my blood sugar goes low and I feel woozy, some water, a small battery pack in case my phone uses a large amount of charge for some unknown reason and some sunscreen – my head is slowly becoming more and more polished!

The interview

- Time to talk turkey! Exchange some pleasantries, ask for a glass of water if you have a dry mouth and then settle into it. Be professional but also approachable, if your feeling super nervous, remember you'll be talking about a shared passion, you've got common ground, so let it flow.

- Expect to talk about your work, your portfolio and your working process. Be ready to answer questions on your art test and what you feel your strengths and weaknesses are.

- Ask about the company's process (if they are willing to share), find out about their pipeline, what software they use and what the artist workflow is like. How editable and flexible are their systems (some pipelines make it difficult to make alterations quickly)?

- Don't badmouth people, projects, or situations. While your grievances may be all true, it's not professional and not appropriate in an interview.

- Don't waffle. You aren't paid by the word so answer the question honestly and with some passion.

- Be truthful. Some questions can be tricky, like 'Why are you leaving your last company?' If you have had a bad experience, it's best to figure out your answers prior to the interview, such as what you want that your current employer isn't providing. Perhaps you seek 'a chance to grow in a different direction', or are 'looking for ways to further your art skills'? There are many ways to turn a poor answer into a positive one. Spend some time on it though!

- Make sure you ask questions; this is just as much about them as it is you.

- Evaluate the room/situation. Is it safe to ask about crunch culture, to find out about the company's views on that and how they deal with it? Do they offer paid overtime? Are meals provided? Would you receive time back in lieu?

- Ensure you ask further questions on company benefits, vacation days, company pension, healthcare, accommodation help and duration.

 Topics of race, sexuality, gender, physical appearance, disability, religion, citizenship, marital status, children are a big no. You are being interviewed on your skills and personality. If you offer them up in the interview, that's ok, but an interviewer should not be asking.

Post-interview

❏ Be appreciative. Make a point of thanking the interviewer for their time, regardless of how the interview has progressed.

❏ Be patient, as some companies are crazily busy. If you've heard nothing after a week, follow up with your point of contact.

Hopefully you were successful! If you were, then it's all change! Time to step up and face a new and exciting challenge. If you weren't so lucky, it's an opportunity for some self-evaluation, to discover areas for improvement before your next application.

THE LOWS OF REJECTION

Nobody likes rejection, especially when your heart is set on a job. When this happens, what can you do to ease the pain of the rejection? Or worse, when the only thing you hear is deafening silence?

I remember my first rejection, I'd applied to Ocean Software, based in Deansgate, Manchester. They had it all, the cool warehouse offices, a quick trip to the bars by the canal, it was good city living. Oh, I really wanted a job, but I knew it was a long shot. My portfolio was woefully light in content. Despite that, I still got an interview, something must have caught their eye. The project was Jurassic Park (1993 version). I didn't get the job; I was pretty clueless about 3D and game pipelines but at the end I grilled my interviewer on hardware and software specs, so determined was I to get my own rig and teach myself after that interview. It was a pivotal point in my career development.

Henry Ford said, 'Failure is only the opportunity to begin again, only this time more wisely'. While I feel that's true, sometimes it's hard to hear straight after losing out on your dream job. But maybe it's too early for sage advice! So, let's look at something more practical and tangible to get you back on track.

1. **Request feedback** – It's now the norm to request feedback on your interview, but if you do this, know that you might get nothing back. Emailing the company, asking if they can provide some insight into why they felt you weren't suitable for the role, is a simple first step. Remember though, that companies must be careful about what and how they reply, so most will steer clear to avoid any legal issues or will provide a generic response.

2. **Moving forwards** – It's time to regroup after the rejection. If you received negative feedback about your application, interview or art test, spend time finding solutions to upgrade your weaknesses. Sure, it's a pain to be rejected, but next time you'll be a stronger candidate, so re-apply for that same role if that truly is your dream job.

 You can apply for a job more than once, but not usually within a six-month timeframe. Make sure you have improved since your last application, as employers will still want to see progression.

The industry can be tough to get into, but if you really want it, it's a matter of staying motivated and proactive. Keep going, keep pushing, keep improving – Go! Go! Go!

SHOW ME THE MONEY

You were accepted? Great, then you're in the last stretch, having reached all the way to the money part. You want to feel appreciated and you want to be comfortable. You don't want to be living in a bedsit with a month's worth of ramen noodles as your only food source. You want to buy coffee, video games and art tutorials, right? Who doesn't! But how do you get paid what you feel you are worth? Some of these factors might help you determine your starting package.

Experience

As a Junior, your experience will be from university or online training. It's possible you've done modding or freelanced prior to your application, all of which bolsters your resume and increases your worth.

Desirability

What sort of artwork are you producing? Some genres are in high demand, so if you are lucky and deliver that type of art, it can benefit you at the negotiation stages. The quality of your work counts too. If you are making killer art, then you are in a strong position to get the salary you want.

Scarcity

Most art positions are environment, because they are the biggest department of the studio and therefore have the most open positions. Roles such as visual effects (VFX) and user interface (UI) have smaller departments, but good candidates are harder to find. Even though they are niche areas, they are just as important as anything else. Quality character artists and concept artists are also scarcer than you would think. My advice would be not to choose a role on scarcity and salary though, rather do what attracts you and what you think you will love, remember, you'll dedicate a large portion of your waking life to this role, choose something that motivates you!

Personal situation

Circumstances play a role in how you operate and negotiate, so if your bank account is about to hit zero, you'll take any job they offer to pay those bills. If you are already in a job (the best circumstance), you are in a safer situation where you can afford to pick, without that weight on your back, bearing down.

> I once resigned from my job and needed a new gig. I wasn't in the best of positions; I had bills to pay, family to support, and I was feeling burnt out. I took the first interesting job I could find, but it meant stepping down my career ladder for a while. That wasn't the worst thing though, a poor exchange rate and lower salaries in the UK meant

> *it paid me 35% less than my previous job. It would never be an easy course of action but looking back at it now, it worked out thankfully ok, I found new routes to progress along and eventually made it to the Art Director role I wanted.*

Salary bands

Companies work with salary bands, which means the way they bracket financial worth per position in the company. Every candidate can be potentially average, good or amazing. Depending on what the project needs, the company will pay X, Y or Z amount. A few websites collate survey data on salaries paid in the US and Europe, so make good use of them to get an idea of how much to expect.

Benefits and bonuses

Often, especially in start-up companies, the salary can be lower if the company wants to conserve funds. They might offer you stock options to make up the perceived shortfall (See 2.4 Show me the goodies). Along with stock options, the benefits package including health, life, dental and pension schemes can also influence your negotiating strategy.

Negotiation

Honestly, in your early career, there isn't much of a negotiation. You need a job and you want to get into the industry, so you're at the disadvantage. While that's the reality of the situation, companies are all in competition with each other. If they want to attract and keep their staff, they'll try to offer attractive packages to keep their workers focused and making games. As you progress in your career, you'll gain a greater ability to negotiate a higher salary, higher-tier bonus package, and other perks.

If you receive a low-ball offer you can still counter, even as a Junior. You can respond with a 'Love the package, but a salary of X amount is what I was hoping for' and see what they say. In the worst case they can say no, it's a final offer, so you'll either take the job or not on that basis. Even better, you might get an increased salary. The middle ground would be an offer to review your salary after six months, and if you prove your worth, they'll honour the increase.

Bonuses are not salary. Salary pays the bills; salary is money in the bank every month. Bonuses are fantasy money, they may happen (and can be big) or they may not, so consider the risks when accepting deals where the salary is low, and the prospect of large bonuses is high. I'm not saying don't do it, just weigh the risk/reward and what that means for you.

THE HIGHS OF SUCCESS

You're on the edge of entering a brave new world, where you can really soar, learning new software and skills while working with exceptional talent. You've about to make a massive leap forward after all the hours of preparation/art tests/interviews, and the effort has paid off. Great job!

But before stepping into this creative arena, is there anything you need to do to wrap your current life up before you embark on your new one?

1. **Arrange your new start date** – Work out how long you want between jobs and whether you can afford it. Do you want some time off or do you want to jump right in and get cracking? Companies are flexible to a certain extent, but if you're serious, don't delay too long, they won't wait forever if there are other candidates to choose from.

2. **Hand in your notice** – Be aware of your current working contract details (if you have one). When handing in your notice to end your current employment, companies and countries operate differently. In the USA it can vary from state to state.

3. **Preliminary paperwork** – Your new employer will email your new contract. Look it over carefully and if you are unsure of anything, seek legal counsel. Note that if you don't like the contract, there's not a lot you can do about it, other than turning down the job offer.

On matters of who owns creative property rights while you're working for them, read the contracts section in 2.1 Gear Up.

4. **Shout from the rooftops** – Let your friends, family and colleagues know about your recent success – it's worth celebrating! Though only post something after all the paperwork is complete.

5. **Time to pack?** – Is your new job in your local area? Great, you don't have to think about packing up and moving. If, like me, you are prepared to move around either in your home country or to a new one, then time to pack and call the movers. Often employers will allocate a moving allowance to take some of the financial strain off you.

RELOCATION

It's likely your new job will involve a move to an unfamiliar place, especially if you have been chasing a specific games company to work with. But you know this already, you applied there and you've done your research because it's been your goal all along.

Relocation to a new country is best suited to a whole different book, because the hoops to jump through and the pitfalls are extensive. If you get the opportunity, I heartily recommend moving; it's challenging but worth it. Even if you have a family in tow, it's totally possible.

Companies may offer relocation packages as part of the offer, often covering flights, transport costs of household contents, visa requirements, lawyers, transport, and temporary accommodation while you find your feet in your new surroundings.

> *At the time of moving to the USA, everyone thought we were crazy. We sold the house, the car, everything, we upped sticks and moved with our three- and five-year-old kids to somewhere we knew next to nothing about. We were about to live the American dream! Nothing*

could have prepared us for the spring pollen levels (cars were turning yellow), the summer heat, my aversion to cockroaches and reaction to mosquito bites! On the flip side, my kids grew up in a safe place, accessed many activities and had a pool and tennis court behind the house, burgers, ice cream and the Epic pantry, meaning free candy and soda when I took them with me.

On reflection, living and working in the States was a once-in-a-lifetime experience. There's nothing quite like travel to expand your mind and horizons, allowing greater understanding of others and different cultures. Developing soft skills and a greater willingness to understand and learn will only help your career, especially if you later choose to progress into management roles such as Lead Artist or Art Director.

LEVEL ONE SUMMARY

Do you know more now than when you started? Do you feel like you have just ingested a large meal and need to lie down? That's ok, rest up and relax while you figure out your game plan. I've put a summary together below to help you focus your thoughts.

1.1 Content preparation

- ❏ Your artwork is the key to getting an interview, is everything as good as it can be?
- ❏ Does your portfolio hit the key beats I outlined from the AD's perspective?
- ❏ Show only your best work, less is more.
- ❏ It's important your work can be seen easily and quickly.
- ❏ Does your resume accurately reflect you and show your passion?
- ❏ Does your cover letter showcase the highlights of your career journey so far?
- ❏ Recruitment agencies can be super helpful if you know what you want.

❏ Art tests aren't mandatory, but if you get one, give yourself time to do your best.

1.2 The interview

❏ Have you done your company/target research?
❏ Are you interview ready and set up for anything that's thrown your way?
❏ Negatives can be turned into positives, and rejection can be good, however bad it feels.
❏ Did you research your salary band and set your expectations?
❏ Got the job? Excellent, let the world know your success!
❏ Moving can be challenging, but it's worth it.

Everyone's journey to finding their gaming destination is different, it happens at different speeds and in different ways. Don't worry if your friend is ahead of you and you are still polishing your portfolio, keep focused and you will get there in your own time.

In **Level Two** you'll get the insider's guide to working in a studio, the settling-in period and an insight into everything you are magically meant to know but never taught. Rather than learning by osmosis, you can simply read it and level up!

LEVEL 02

JUNIOR ARTIST

YOUR BIG BREAK

This is it! All your hard work has paid off and you've got the gig that you always wanted. All the research, the homework, the extra polish, the blood, sweat and tears, and even a few failures (learning experiences) along the way have finally culminated in getting your foot in the door of the elusive gaming industry.

Are you feeling a mix of excitement, enthusiasm and nervousness? I know I was. Fear not! This is natural, you want to do your best, make a good impression, and not feel like an idiot if you do something 'wrong', but you really don't know what you are going to face, day-to-day in the coming year.

You may be asking yourself, who do I listen to? How much work should I be doing? How can I impress my manager? How do I negotiate a pay raise? Well, hold onto your hat, it's a bit early to be talking about more money at this stage, but you'll find out the answers to these questions and more later on.

Level Two lays out the fundamentals of game dev life; I want to set you up with the basics before you launch into your career.

This chapter builds the foundation to launch your career. I've gone wide to introduce a broad slice of the world you've just entered. Some may argue that it's too much information too soon, but I think that preparation is the key. You'll find a treasure trove of information to set you firmly in the right direction.

We'll delve into what's expected of you as a person and as a growing professional. We look at your induction and what the first months might be like, and the company structure, to identify the movers and shakers in the organisation. We examine the game development pipeline, team structure and how tasks are generated. After looking at the company, we look closer at the influencing forces, how to cope with stress (it's your first gig, so some stress is natural), and keeping on top of your health. You'll realise that, from day one, you are a professional and that high standards are expected.

Finally, we cover money, perks and benefits. These often seem confusing or complex, so I help demystify what's on offer and how to take full advantage. Get a drink and snack, we're going on a strange adventure as we enter the world of the game artist!

2.1 GEAR UP

2.2 ONWARDS AND UPWARDS

2.3 KEEP CALM AND CARRY ON

2.4 SHOW ME THE GOODIES

LEVEL
2.1

GEAR UP

WHAT'S A JUNIOR ARTIST?

Being a Junior Artist is one of the most exciting times in your career; it's a brave unknown world and one of concentrated learning. At the moment, you aren't sure of how you'll progress, where you'll excel, how fast you'll rise and what mistakes you'll make, but that's ok, it's all part of the journey.

You're not on your own, as you'll read in this chapter, you'll be working as part of a team. You might be part of a massive corporate machine or a small focused indie unit; it doesn't really matter. What matters is you're now an important part of the games industry.

Those countless hours you spent crafting away at every nut, bolt, pixel, and polygon for your portfolio will have served you well, giving you an insight into the role, but until you actually start working in the studio, you won't know for sure. But you'll find out quickly. The team is there to support you and you'll be up to speed before you know it!

How it works

- ❑ Your manager is the Lead Artist, who oversees your workload and tasking.

- ❑ The Art Director (AD) is your indirect manager, they'll concentrate on your artwork.

- ❑ Your tasks start small and easy to digest, to build confidence.

- ❑ You are given time to learn the pipeline, to make assets for the game engine.

- ❑ Don't be afraid of offering ideas or asking questions.

- ❑ You'll be eager to work, but don't overdo it and focus on pacing yourself.

What you learn here in your first art role and how you implement it will influence the direction of your career path. There's always a steep learning curve on entering the industry, but don't worry, you've already got to this point. Now it's a matter of learning, implementing, reflecting, and continuing to improve. It's a long time since I was a Junior, but getting to every position had two things in common, commitment and hard work.

Other chapters show how I made my way up to Art Director, and from others as they progressed in the industry too, so rest assured you're not alone on this journey.

SLICE OF LIFE – JUNIOR ARTIST INSIGHT

Now take a breath and read these sage words from Amber as she recollects her time as a Junior Artist working for a UK games studio. In the time it took me to write this book, she's become a Senior Artist. Before you know it, you'll be well on your way, too.

Q. Before we dive in, tell me your name, your current title and your time in the industry so far.

A. My name is Amber Marie Edwards, I'm a 3D Artist who has been in the industry now for six years. I was Junior Artist for about 11 months before being promoted to Artist (Mid).

Q. Let's take a step back in time, to your junior days. What's the overall feeling of your first days in the industry? Was it a heady mix of fear and excitement?

A. To start with it was certainly fear. I had to learn a new software in two weeks and I honestly thought for a long time I was doing things wrong and was going to mess up completely. I thought those first few months they would let me go because in my eyes I was making so many mistakes and was quite clueless. I didn't realise it was ok for me not to know everything straight away, but the people on my team honestly helped me stop feeling that way. Fear turned into excitement after the first couple of months, and I just wanted to learn more and make more.

Q. What were your biggest surprises in the games industry for your first months leading up to your first year? Was it work, people, process, culture?

A. The biggest surprise was how different it was from my time at university. Nothing prepared me for the big difference from just casually learning bits and pieces to full on in-game development and learning a company's ways. That honestly was the real starting point to kicking off learning in and outside of work. The amount of knowledge I gained in that first year was incomprehensible. Thankfully, I had a great team to help me deal with that and encourage me as projects went. They gave me all the support and knowledge I needed, when I would make mistakes, they'd help me realise it's ok and teach me how to avoid making those mistakes. Another surprise was I didn't expect all the people I had contact with to be so kind, patient and helpful, I was quite an anxious person and they helped me with managing that.

Q. What advice would you give to your starter self, something that could have helped your entry into the industry?

A. Amber; just breathe! It's ok, you can make mistakes, no one will make you feel bad for them. Learning takes time and patience. You don't have to be perfect, you're not as annoying as you think you are. Your team and the people you work with are more than happy answering your questions, so don't feel you can't go ask them for help! That's another piece of advice I'd like to give those of you reading. If you don't know something and can't find a solution, go ask! You're not bothering anyone in asking for help.

Q. Where do you see yourself in five years – you've got a plan, right?

A. In five years, I'm hoping maybe I'll be a Lead or Principal Artist by then. I had dreams of becoming an Art Director one day, it's tough out there but with a lot of learning and gaining more experience it will be interesting to see where I'll be. All I know is I want to be someone that encourages the people I work around to make the best art they can. I want to give back the support I once had as a Junior to the future artists we have coming up and if I'm doing that, that's more than enough for me.

Amber Marie Edwards
https://www.artstation.com/amb3re

WORDS OF ADVICE

Imagine your adventure is to climb a great mountain, say, Mount Everest. You've studied the map, lined up a Sherpa guide, booked the flights, and bought many bits of kit and supplies for the trip. You name it; you have it, and you would take the kitchen sink if you could.

But, like any great expedition, the preparation is just the start. Of course, your actual journey won't be as dramatic as Figure 2 and you won't have a 'death zone', but my goal is to help you to your summit with the minimum of drama.

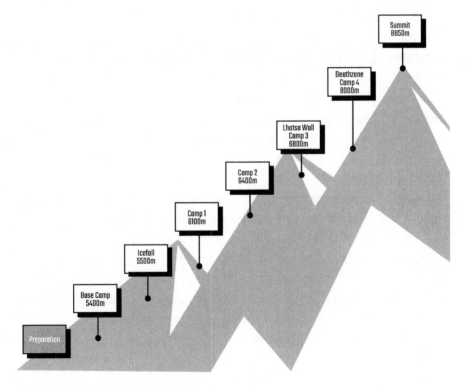

Figure 2. The stages of climbing Everest

I'd like to start by impressing on you a couple of points because, with these thoughts in mind, you'll find working in the games industry makes more sense earlier on. Your path to the summit will be a little easier emotionally and psychologically.

You're making a commercial product

At the end of the day, a video game is a commercial product. It provides income for investing back into the company as salaries, bonuses, rent, equipment, soda, chips, and marketing, among many other things. Generating income provides a future for everyone who works in the company and the many other stakeholders who rely upon it.

There's a chain of command

Love or hate authority, companies have a chain of command. You have a boss; your boss has a boss, and so on. Bosses affect your career in that they can give you a leg-up or they can block your progress. Understand that from day one, and you start to understand the system.

Companies generate more work than they can complete

In the creative industries, producing quality artwork while developing technology is a constant balancing act. Companies push for as much as they can get from a team because they want the best product they can create. How you balance this workload is down to you.

Work-life balance

You alone take care of yourself. You're responsible for the effort and time you put into the workplace. If you work 12 hours a day voluntarily, will you have the energy when the project needs you to crunch? Companies are improving, and trying to eliminate the overspill of work, but not all are doing it and not all at the same rate. The responsibility falls on you to keep on top of your mental and physical health. You wouldn't think twice about watching a new tutorial about artwork, but what about attending to your wellbeing with the same devotion?

Prepare for some hiccups

It's important not to see failure as a negative, so try to frame in your mind that it's part of the process. Be prepared to make mistakes because making them is natural, but the important lesson for your growth is how you learn and recover from those mistakes.

The long haul

Consider how far and how fast you want to run this race. Remember, this is a marathon of sorts, not a sprint. Some of your peers will be ahead of you, some behind, so don't worry about them, and instead focus on yourself and what you can do to improve your situation. Identify the areas where you feel most vulnerable and look to bolster them. Make use of tutorials, friends, or other professionals for example, whatever works for you, but some things can't be rushed. Sometimes, it's down to experience, and time is the only thing that provides that.

Before we rush in to meet the team and understand the company, there's the matter of the paperwork and contracts. Not everything in game dev life is flashy and attractive, but these documents and details, while dull, are important!

CONTRACT AND POLICY

I'm not one for reading legalese (legal jargon) but it's a necessary first step before you rock up to the company ready to do your bit for the next great game. Facing a wall of text, paragraphs, subsections and lawyer-speak can be intimidating, so it's natural to want to sign on the dotted line and make it go away. However, let me give you a few pointers.

Working Time Directive

In the UK, you can choose to work more than the maximum 48-hour week. We call this 'opting out'. You can't be forced to opt out, but you'll be asked if you're willing to do so. Unfortunately, this is standard practice in the games industry, and it means that you're prepared to work the hours required to get the job done (this is what we know as crunch).

It begs the question, 'What happens if I don't opt out, will it affect my career?' Honestly, I don't know, because I don't know anyone who hasn't opted out. We all keep marching to the drum, working away to complete the game.

Creative rights ownership

You'll want to look for this in your employment contract. Often a contract will specify that any work an employee creates while working there belongs to the company. So, you could make a cool mini game project or an artistic endeavour in your apartment in your spare time, but technically, that work would belong to the company, not you. If, on the other hand, you have a prior written agreement specifying you are the copyright holder, your hard work and creativity remain in your control. You may already be familiar with this from university, as it's common practice to own the student's intellectual property.

Non-Disclosure Agreement (NDA)

An NDA exists to prevent you from releasing information about the company, people or projects. Breaching your agreement can result in being fired or worse, a lawsuit. If and when you leave a company, you'll be expected to return any company goods (notebooks, hard drives, schedules, etc) so that sensitive information can't be leaked.

Non-compete clause

Contracts can include a clause that is known as a non-compete clause. It often means that, if you leave the job, you can't work for a competitor for a set amount of time. They're less common for junior roles, but as you climb the ladder are worth watching out for.

Those are some quirks that might appear in your contract. Most of it will be straightforward and simple enough to read and understand without a lawyer, however, if you feel unsure, seek legal advice.

As well as contract terms such as start date, hours, salary, duration, dismissal, I want to highlight a few areas that will affect you daily as part of company policy.

Paid time off

As part of keeping a healthy body and a healthy mind, paid time off (PTO) factors heavily in your wellbeing and keeping in tip-top shape for when those tough times arrive. Yet different countries vary on how much time should be given per year. Compared to the US, the UK is more generous in the number of days off given for vacation.

Some companies are adopting 'unlimited time off', the idea being to provide the employee with more choice for work/life balance. However, some companies found that staff were actually taking less time off and felt more anxious without a limit. They also felt pressure to not take holiday if their co-workers weren't, and high performers stayed high performing and took less time off. What works for one organisation or individual might not work for another.

Sick days

Everyone gets sick, it happens to the best of us. Policies like paid time off (PTO), sick days are treated differently depending on the country, so know what your country's or state's regulations are.

 It's vital you do your homework when signing up to work with a new company. Not only do you want to know you're getting the best deal, but also that you're not being boxed into a corner, especially if you have ideas of a side project.

HUMAN RESOURCES (HR)

This is the first department of the company you'll interact with, and this department handles the development and management of employees, among other things.

To make the best use of HR it's important to understand what they deal with, including:

- **Recruitment and staffing** – employment contracts, on-boarding, and off-boarding (hiring and firing)

- **Employee relations** – a wide swath of things related to people working with other people and all that can entail, both good and bad

- **Training and learning** – personal, team, department, and whole-company training

- **Workplace/organisation development** – personal development, staff reviews and corporate wellbeing

- **Compensation and benefits** – pension, bonuses, healthcare, and social events, among many other things

In your early years, you'll have little interaction with this department after your induction. When you become a team leader and above, you'll find that you work with them more and more as your team gets larger and your tasks become more complex. Your first experience will be HR settling you in, which includes a tour of the facilities, showing you to your workspace and introducing you to your manager. Along with that, you will need to complete the paperwork to provide the company with your personal and financial information so you can get paid.

Bring the essentials

The usual forms of ID, such as passport or driving licence, National Insurance (UK) or Social Security Number (USA), and bank details for remuneration are required. In the US, payment is often every two weeks while in the UK, it's monthly.

Now the essentials are out the way, let's move onto finding out more about company life and how you'll fit into the organisation.

LEVEL 2.2

ONWARDS
AND UPWARDS

ON PROBATION

Most games jobs have a probation period, no matter how much of a hot shot you are. This is standard procedure to protect both you and your new employer, almost acting as an extended job interview. You'll have an initial settling-in period, during which your workload is relatively light so you can acclimatise to your new workplace, project and people. Art tasks are eventually assigned to you to contribute to the project, and before you know it, you are on your way to making your first commercial video game.

This period is your opportunity to show your new employer how good you are. It's also where your company evaluates whether you're doing what they expect and in the way they like it. Probation periods, nine times out of ten, are straightforward, and these are the things they will look for:

- Achieving goals set by the Lead Artist

- Meeting the core values of the organisation, including in terms of your behaviour

- Turning up to work on time and working the expected hours

- Communication skills and integration with the team

- Listening and feedback skills

Your manager (Lead Artist) over this period provides rolling feedback, giving you gentle nudges to get you up to speed. This is a two-way street. It's also an opportunity for you to work out any kinks that you have, things you know are tripping you up or slowing down your natural pace. Initially, it can feel you are trying to work with boxing gloves on, everything feels different, even your favourite software.

How long does it last?

Different countries have different procedures, but there is a lot of common ground. Having worked full time only in the UK and the USA, I include both for reference. The UK is typically three to six months, the USA, 90 days, but it's company dependent and isn't state or nationally mandated.

Can I get fired in my probation period?

Technically, yes. However, to avoid a case of unfair dismissal, your manager will have to have given you reasonable feedback to implement, which you will have failed to achieve. If you commit something serious such as racism, sexism, dangerous behaviour, theft or violence, then yes, expect to be out of a job that day.

What happens at the end of the probation period?

You'll be notified at a meeting and they will confirm via email which of the three outcomes applies to you. The options are passed, failed, or extended.

❏ **Pass** – congratulations, you are now officially part of the club!

❏ **Fail** – you pick up your box of things and may even be escorted out via security.

❏ **Extend** – requires you to fix your problems within a set period and be re-evaluated.

 If this happens to you and your probation is extended, take it seriously. Look to fix the issues outlined by your boss/company, go the extra mile if possible. You must be 'that person' that really turned things around.

SETTLING IN

It's often a little awkward starting somewhere new. New equipment, new environment, new people. It's intimidating at first, but you'll find out you're surrounded by other caring creatives and they all know that first-day feeling.

Common practice, and one of the simplest ways of settling someone into the company, is to assign them a buddy. Your Lead will have picked someone from the team to help you out, someone you can turn to who'll ease your transition into the world of game development. On the off chance that no one has been picked to help you settle in, my advice would be to start with the friendliest artist you've met so far and go from there!

Groundwork

With everything in place and now sitting at your new workstation, you'll be ready to input the plethora of logins and passwords required for all the new software you need to get started.

Take the time to read all the information you can. There will be details about the company including a new starters' pack to help you orientate yourself with the company and the building/area. There should be documentation on the game, too. I say should, because often game documents are the last element to be updated by staff and so they can be out of date. The more you know at the start, the better prepared you will be. It's not a test though, so no need to go overboard on your first day.

Settling in

I'm a self-confessed hermit, whereas you might be the opposite and find socialising easy. If you do, I envy you! Regardless, in your first week, dedicate time to finding out more about your team and surroundings. From what I've experienced, lunchtimes, especially in the USA, are a daily social event, while in the UK, they seem less so. Staff tend to get lunch and bring it back to their desks with Friday or the last day of the month being a time to gather for food and drinks, either at lunch or after hours.

 Never be afraid to ask questions, but be sure to listen to the answers given. Write down the details, especially if, like me, you have a 64Kb memory.

COMPANY STRUCTURE

So, you're at your cool new desk, you've met the team, your new boss, you know where the important things like the muffins, coffee machine and bathroom are, but where in the larger scheme of things do you fit? How does the team function? Who decides what the team works on? And what happens if you run out of snacks?! (That last one is a joke, sort of.)

Depending on the scale of the operation, companies will structure themselves slightly differently. We'll be looking at a simplified, typical set-up in Figure 3 to give you an idea of where you are on the corporate ladder.

Figure 3. Example of a typical game studio corporate ladder

Publisher – If your company has a publisher (some self-publish), they provide the funding for the project. As part of an agreement, they'll provide support to make sure the game is hitting its targets, visually, fiscally and in terms of timeframe. Not all publishers are the same (this won't be the first time you'll hear this caveat); some are heavily involved in development and like to micromanage, some are hands off and don't interfere with the creative vision.

Executive team – The team making the big decisions. It's normally a bunch of chiefs – Chief Executive Officer (CEO), Chief Financial Officer (CFO), Chief Technical Officer (CTO), Chief Operating Officer (COO), President and Creative Director to name a few. This team is working to keep the company's vision on track along with the development of the project.

Directors – The senior staff. Directors work alongside each other to get the best for their team and the game. For you, the artist, your director is the Art Director (AD).

Development team – This includes you, plus everyone else involved in making the game, all the way from junior to the top, before hitting director level.

From this high-level view of the organisation shown in Figure 4, we'll now slowly zoom in, focusing on the structure of an art team and how they operate as part of the company.

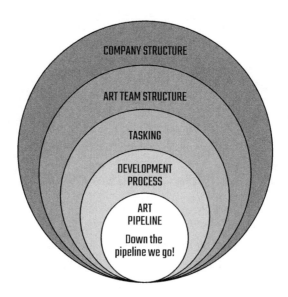

Figure 4. Game development pipeline, from *corporate* structure all the way down to *game asset* process

ART TEAM STRUCTURE

You know the typical company structure now, but what makes up an art team? What artistic disciplines are available and what proportion of artists make up the development team? Artists make up a sizeable proportion of a company's dev team, because expectations for quality and quantity of artwork are high.

I'm covering a typical hierarchy here, with one Art Director (AD) for the project. Where organisations have multiple game studios, it's not uncommon to have a Global Art Director overseeing different projects. And where the project is vast and complex, it's possible to have multiple ADs covering each major artistic discipline.

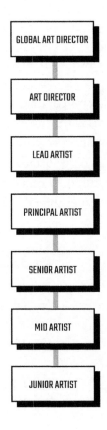

Figure 5. Art team structure

Figure 5 shows how the art team is split in terms of seniority, and you'll find a more detailed explanation of each position later on. This is just to become familiar with titles and hierarchy.

- Junior Artist (welcome to the club)

- Mid Artist (eager for more)

- Senior Artist (heavy lifting artist)

- Principal Artist (art kickass)

- Lead Artist (kicks your ass)

- Art Director (responsible for everything art-related on that game)

- Global Art Director (high level with an overview of multiple games)

The art team comprises a collection of unique departments, so the bigger the team, the more specialisms within it. When studios run with smaller teams, often artists take on multiple roles, and their job descriptions may be split into definitions such as hard surface artist (weapons, props, vehicles, mechanical, architectural), or organic artist (trees, geological formations, flora, and fauna) rather than the more typical granular departments listed below:

- Concept
- Characters
- Environment
- Lighting
- Props

- Weapons
- Vehicle
- VFX (Visual Effects)
- UI/UX (User Interface, User Experience)

Figure 6 illustrates four games companies I've worked for previously. You can clearly see how environment artists normally account for the largest section of the art department. If you're reading this section as someone looking to join the industry, environment art always has multiple positions open. The flipside is that new artists often are training up in this area, so competition remains high within the industry.

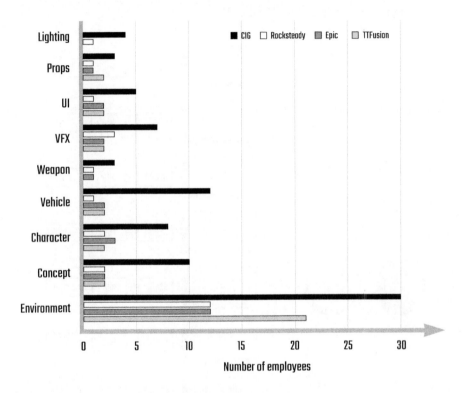

Figure 6. Example of art department staff numbers per discipline

The following four areas sometimes come under an Art Director's remit, but can also have their own directors and can be completely separate departments:

❑ Animation ❑ Marketing/Promotion

❑ Cinematics ❑ Tech art

Team structure examples

The type of project, size and how it's been run historically all factor into the type of team organisation. I've jotted down three examples that I've worked with.

The first involves the Art Director and Lead Artist overseeing the whole art team regardless of discipline (Figure 7).

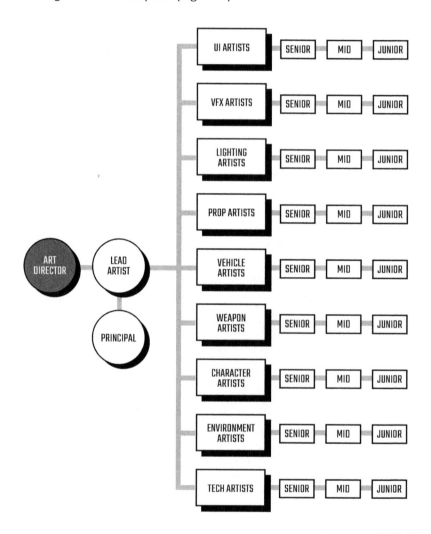

Figure 7. Team structure V1

In this second structure (in Figure 8), the AD has multiple leads, some with a Principal Artist embedded within their subsection.

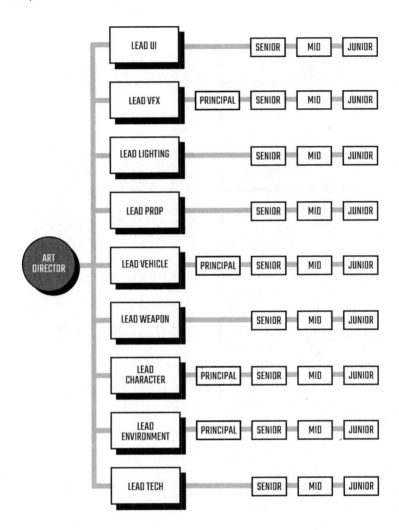

Figure 8. Team structure V2

In the final structure (see Figure 9), ADs would oversee multiple areas and some ADs (environment) would have multiple leads taking on different parts of the world. All directors here would report to the Creative Director.

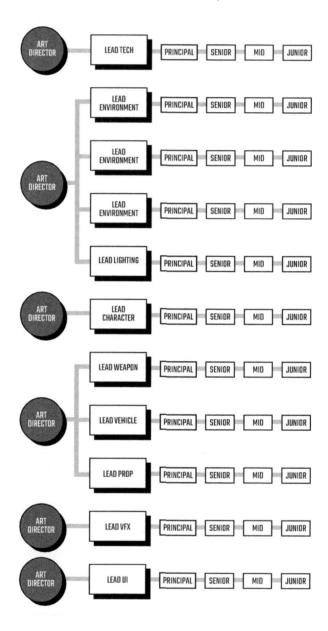

Figure 9. Team structure V3

If you haven't already figured it out, the games industry is quite fluid in how it works. Nothing is set in stone and companies tend to work in a variety of ways. There's no 'perfect way' and plenty of artists will have experienced structures not illustrated here, but my aim is to at least give you an idea. Chances are that your company has documentation that shows the company structure and illustrates who answers to whom if you're unsure.

Regardless of structure, all the disciplines have a career path and a ladder to climb, taking you up through the positions I mentioned at the start of this chapter.

It's worth noting that you can transfer between departments. You aren't stuck for life in your area of specialisation, however, to transfer you'll need to show proof of your skills and show current and prospective boss that you have the attitude and aptitude to make the jump.

For example, if you build assets for environments and you want to be a character artist, I'd expect to see examples of character work that you have done in your spare time. You won't impress anyone if you have nothing to bring to the table but live in a fantasy world of 'Oooh, I want to make characters, they look cooler than environments'.

 Remember that you're selling yourself; proving to your next Lead Artist/Art Director that you are worth the risk. Get feedback on your work before showing it to your prospective boss.

TASKING

So, where do tasks originate? Maybe this sounds a bit stupid, but I think it's a valid question. When you're working as part of the art team, it can seem like being in *Charlie and the Chocolate Factory*, a world where tasks magically appear and you have no idea how they came about, their frequency, and who is making the calls.

It's essentially a simple trickle-down system; ideas and desires originate at the top and flow down to the development team. However, it's not a straight fall, the process is more nuanced with gates that require review, so that chaos doesn't rain down on the team. Figure 10 is a version of the process to give you an idea of a typical set-up.

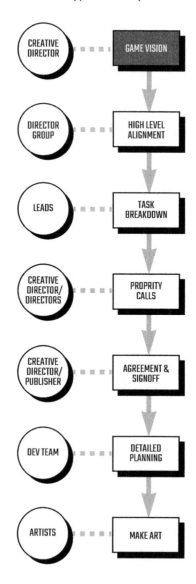

Figure 10. Decision making, planning and tasking

I'll go through these stages and explain them in more detail, so it's clear who does what and why.

Game vision – Set by the Creative Director (CD) who is the visionary for the game. They're the initial driving force to building out the game, considering all high-level aspects of the project including core gameplay loops, design, visuals, audio and cinematics for example, and how they'll tie together.

High-level alignment – Each department's directors work with their teams and other departments to help define, focus and develop the CD's vision to agree what's possible, make sure they are all aligned, and know what's expected.

Task breakdown – The Leads and Producers take the high-level vision and break it down into smaller groups. Often the project is defined as a series of features and within those features, a myriad of tasks. If the Lead's group is seasoned, they can do the breakdowns themselves, if not, they'll take input from their teams to fully understand the scope and timeframes for each of those features.

Priority calls – Part of this is building scenarios. It's no use to come up with just plan A, you need to come up with Plans B and C. These plans are options to be discussed; how to get the game made with factors such as feature priority, staffing, time frame and budget.

Agreement and sign-off – The CD signs off the master plan of action. If the company has a publishing company which is paying for the project, then they'll also be part of the sign-off (or rejection) process.

Detailed planning – Let's say Plan B was chosen, it's now down to the feature teams to drill down further and define the work involved at a more granular level. A feature team will be made of mixed disciplines (design, code, art, etc) and seniority (Juniors to Leads). They'll basically break down tasks and work quotas to fill a three-month block of time (quarterly).

Make art – Start feature development. In short, take your task, start making artwork!

This breakdown seems relatively straightforward, however, it takes an enormous amount of work and team collaboration to bring all estimates together. So much so, in fact, dedicated software is used to track all the estimates, dependencies, and milestones. Companies use a range of project planning software, from off-the-shelf solutions (Microsoft Project or even Excel) to custom dedicated systems, providing the organisation with in-depth analysis and tracking of a game's progress.

DEVELOPMENT PROCESS

Making games follows a formula, or perhaps it's more of a recipe. Companies know the ingredients needed to make a game, but how they mix them together is the difference between success and failure. Add a sprinkling of the magic ingredient called fun, and you have a winning combination. But it's far from an exact science.

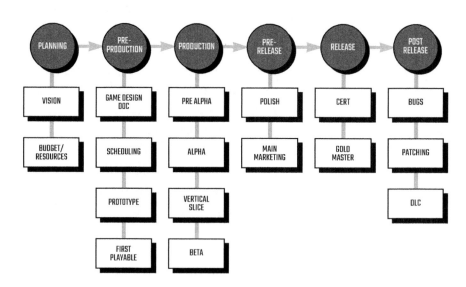

Figure 11. Game development process

On talking through this process with a colleague, it became clear there's a lot of variation in the industry here too. Factors such as size of studio, new game or a sequel, start-up company or large multinational, all tweak the recipe depending on their needs. You could spend a whole evening debating the ideal process, so I'm giving you a pipeline based on what I've experienced (see Figure 11), but ultimately where you end up working could be quite different.

To me, it's preferable to start the game-making process small and contained, growing and adding to the team as you become more confident of the game's direction. Let's go through the stages and I'll explain more as we progress.

Planning

Both exciting and scary, especially if it's a brand-new game. As we saw in 'Tasking', it involves the Creative Director and senior staff defining the vision for the project, which will help the overall planning and development of the game.

It's easy to get carried away with grand visions, to over scope and underestimate the complexity of crucial features for the game, however, without a crystal ball it's difficult to see where your challenges will come from.

With a strong, experienced team at the helm, the risks are lower but don't be under any illusion, at best it's still an educated guess.

The variables under consideration in this part of the pipeline are:

- **Budget** – how much can the company or publisher afford to invest?

- **Genre** – racing, adventure, fighting, puzzle, etc

- **Features** – what's the hook of the game, what will draw players in?

- **Team size** – how many, how soon, when to ramp up, outsource?

- **Target platform** – PC, VR, console, mobile

- **Time frame** – the time allocated dictates the size/quality of the project

- **Monetisation** – ways of boosting sales and further increasing revenue in the long term

Pre-production

With the planning information in hand, developers can start work on the new project, which is best described as the heavy exploration phase of the project. You know what you want to achieve, but you aren't sure how.

A studio must show the publisher (if you have one), the executives and the dev team what the company is striving to build. This stage is very fluid, with changes happening in pursuit of finding the fun. What happens in pre-production sets the direction for the project going forward. Let me break this important stage down some more:

- **Game design document (GDD)** – A living document, detailing the direction of the game and a guiding vision to the rest of the development team. It's in constant revision, hence the term 'live'. Inside, you'll find the grand vision, examples of gameplay style, reference art, game mechanics, everything needed to bring this game to life.

- **Scheduling** – After the vision comes the planning. Sounds simple, but I'm sure producers will tell you it's like herding a bunch of cats. Chasing down directors and leads, getting estimates, figuring out dependencies and getting sign-offs before the pre-production team can start work.

- **Prototype** – Where the work starts. Developers must find efficient ways of building rough individual new game features, like destructible vehicles, flying cars, shooting nano-goop, hacking security systems. Each of these areas is built up with the aim of joining them together.

- **First playable** – Here's where the features I just mentioned are all held together with the equivalent of string and tape. It's crashy, buggy and best described as 'rough', but it sort of works, enough to give the studio an idea of where the gold is.

Production

I once heard someone say, 'If you don't know how the game is going to be built or how it's going to play, then you're still in pre-production'. Once you pass this milestone, you enter production mode. Full-on content creation and collaboration takes place as the development team works to build out the remainder of the game.

Planning and estimating the rest of the game is quite a task, so companies use a method of project management known as Agile to organise the hundreds of tasks that make the game shippable. Within that, Scrum complements the Agile framework, enabling teams to work on smaller bite-sized pieces of the game, adapting to any new information such as changes in technology, design or code, ultimately moving one step closer to the final product.
https://blog.bydrec.com/a-comprehensive-comparison-between-the-agile-scrum-and-waterfall-methodology

Full production of a game happens over years, with constant iterative improvements. Since making games isn't an exact science, there'll be times when work is redone multiple times while the gameplay is refined and honed. New IPs are notoriously hard to develop, often taking over six years to finish. Sequel games, on the other hand, often use existing technology and provide a quicker and smoother process, taking two-to-three years from what I've experienced.

The production cycle includes these stages. However, I spoke with three different producers, and they all had slightly different understandings of these stages, so I've gone with the one that made most sense to me! I'm an artist – don't judge me!

- ❑ **Pre-Alpha** – The stage where the game is playable and ready for wider testing. It's still very much the bare bones of a game, but the team has the opportunity for a larger feedback loop, enabling more refinement of game tech and gameplay.

- **Alpha** – Is considered 'feature complete'. It'll be full of bugs and crashes, but it's all there. In an ideal world, this also means no extra features can go in (if they do, it's known as feature creep). Alpha is a critical stage for testing, to give the towering pile of code and assets a good stress test, to really find out what's stable and what could come crashing down (in a digital sense). As issues and crashes arise (this is normal) they're assigned to a bug-tracking database. Bugs are assigned different levels of severity and an order of priority. If something is a game breaker, then it must be fixed as soon as possible, to avoid holding up the development team. Testing is undertaken by quality assurance (QA), the relentless task of playing, finding and logging bugs into the database. This can also be where the public is first introduced to the game.

- **Vertical slice (VS)** – In our example, it happens here in the process pipeline. Some companies implement VS earlier in the pre-production phase, especially if publishers are making 'go, no go' decisions about the viability of a game idea.

But what's a VS I hear you ask?! Good question (cue Figure 12).

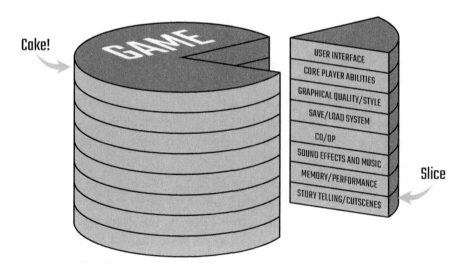

Figure 12. Vertical slice

Imagine the total game as a huge, layered cake. That's one enormous cake and in terms of development (cooking time) it's going to take years to make it all. The risk is ending up with a game that's overcooked, bitter tasting and ugly. So, to mitigate risk, you just bake one slice. It contains everything it needs, but is small and manageable.

This generates a playable demo, somewhere between 10-30 minutes in length that gives the player a good idea of the final product. It's not final, it just feels final.

- **Beta** – Content and FX are locked, with some departments having a little more wiggle room before going into lockdown. By this point, the game is pretty much there. The team has worked thousands of hours to bring this massive project to a playable state.

The game is now ready for more extensive player testing and feedback, while in the background the dev team continues fixing carefully vetted issues. You don't want to be that person who changes an asset which causes the game to crash!

Beta can have two stages, closed and open. Closed Beta is invitation-only for testing the game. Open Beta is like open hunting season, the public are invited to play (and break) the game. It's great for stress testing the product and finding out how players behave in this universe.

Pre-release – Now we're approaching the last stages, we can split them in two:

- **Polish** – As it sounds, this is the fixing of any remaining issues based on the Beta testing, addressing any network issues, performance, showstoppers, blue screen of death, etc.

- **Marketing** – The main campaign rolls out. There will have been hints all along the development process, but publishers won't commit to a full advertising campaign until they're certain it'll hit its final dates.

Release – Approaching the finish line and quickly, the game is done, and now tested by the publisher on the correct platform (console or PC, etc).

- ❏ **Release candidate(s)** – As mentioned, a build of the game the developer considers complete. It's common for multiple release candidates to be submitted, as they can often fail based on a technical issue. On failing, the developer makes the required fixes and resubmits another candidate.

- ❏ **Gold** – In the past, this used to be Gold Master. When the final release candidate was successful, it would be (and still is) duplicated onto discs. However, with games selling as digital downloads on platforms such as Valves Steam and the Epic Games Store, or the console's own content delivery system, 'going gold' means it's ready to be deployed and made available to players.

Post-release – Once the game is delivered and gamers playing, it's back to work for some departments.

- ❏ **Bugs** – It's not uncommon for bugs still to exist even after roll-out (I'm sure you've experienced it). Developers will carefully pick which issues to fix to improve the gaming experience, such as art, code, networking, any manner of issue.

- ❏ **Patching** – You may have heard of a day-one patch? Think of it as a sticking plaster for the game. Downloaded and installed, it contains fixes completed in the time between 'going gold' and being installed on the player's system. Patches are often ongoing through the life of the game, incrementally refining it each time.

- ❏ **Downloadable content (DLC)** – Additional content for the game, released after the main title. It can be free or paid, small (new weapons, characters, skins, etc) or large (new maps to explore, missions, campaigns to complete).

In a nutshell, that's a high-level view of game development. So, you might think, ok, that's interesting and all, but what about the art bit, where do I fit in to this process? Let's look at the art pipeline and the jigsaw should start to piece together.

ART PIPELINE

As an artist you'll experience different parts of the art pipeline. A Junior Artist's path is relatively simple, at least in the early days, while you're figuring things out. On projects, the Senior Artists tend to work on the more complex content and heavy lifting, including pre-production tasks, look development and technical hurdles. As problems are solved, the information is passed down to the rest of the team. This way, you spend your time creating quality assets and less of it worrying about the tech/process.

I'm not going to talk about art pipelines in the sense of how to take an asset from zero to final art. That's often specific to each studio and the overall process is well documented (how to make a character, prop, weapon, etc) on the internet. I want instead to give you a bird's eye view of how the art department works, how an asset is conceived and how it travels along, developing and eventually shipping in line with the process we've just read.

- ❏ **Planning**
  - ❏ Reference and vision

- ❏ **Pre-production art**
  - ❏ Look development
  - ❏ Prototype
  - ❏ Asset pipeline development

- **Production art**
  - Art vertical slice
  - Making art
  - White box
  - Grey box
  - Final art
  - Optimisation
  - Bug fixing

- **Pre-release**
  - Polish

- **Release**
  - Downtime

- **Post-release**
  - Downloadable content

Planning – While the Creative Director and team works out what the new game should be, the Art Director (AD) will make their own choices, feeling out new ideas and how to create something fresh and exciting.

- **Reference and vision** – The AD collates ideas to create a vision board that defines the direction for the new game. It used to mean finding and printing images and sticking them on the wall, and some may still do that (it livens up the office). Now digital whiteboards and software enable you to collate all your ideas in one space, which is infinitely more accessible, shareable and collaborative. Part of the process also involves research on your competitors; what they do well, what to avoid accidentally copying and how to leapfrog ahead of them.

  One of the vital parts is defining the 'visual hook'; what makes the game or the artwork memorable, what's going to hook the player's attention? Technology and processing power all play their part in decision making too. As the tech advances, so do the creative options.

Pre-production art – In step with rest of the team, with initial planning over, it's onto pre-production. Remember that GDD (Game Design Document)? Well, that's already being created, and in unison, the AD is also creating the beginnings of the continuously evolving Art Bible. These documents provide the direction for a clear initial vision for the art team. As a Junior, it's unlikely you'll experience the pre-production part of game development (it's not unknown though), which is normally tackled by a hit squad of experienced artists. Your AD will want to rapidly iterate on ideas, and with a team of heavy hitters, they can make visual leaps faster and further, which is ideal at this stage.

❑ **Look development** – With a basic game design brief to work with, the AD and concept team can really let their imaginations run wild, especially on a new IP. New ideas are quickly visualised, it's an enjoyable process of discovery where boundaries and limitations are few. Of course, it's not carte blanche, the art has to support the Creative Director's vision and gameplay, but the AD's job is to push the thinking into fresh territory.

❑ **Prototype** – This art team provides assets quickly to support the game team as they experiment with ideas and prove out theories for gameplay. The artwork can best be described as rough and rapid, it may look good to the casual eye, but behind the scenes it's often highly unoptimised. Tentative steps are taken to translate the concept art into game art, sometimes known as a beautiful corner. A section of a room, landscape or city, a visual prototype is assembled in the game editor. It might use old assets or ones from a library, the objective is to achieve exciting new visuals that support gameplay.

❑ **Asset pipeline development** – In tandem with the prototype, the pre-production team will assess how new assets are constructed, identifying if there's any new tech or tools required so that when the project progresses to full production, the main pool of artists can work seamlessly and unhindered. It's never that simple though! In reality, pre-production work bleeds over and the pipeline is in constant development, especially for new IPs.

Production art – This is the turning on the tap, where the art team works on the game at full flow, building out areas of the game based on the results of the previous visual experiments.

❑ **Vertical Slice** – The art VS tries to solve a good cross section of the new game, each layer (remember that layer cake?) with specific challenges to solve. The slice of cake involves a variety of art assets and, while the temptation is to create something from start to finish and then test, it's too risky. Work can easily be wasted and development time increased, which is why we use stages.

❑ **Making art** – An art asset will travel through four key stages in its lifetime, White box (first pass), Grey box (second pass), Final Art and optimisation. This helps reduce the risk of wasted work. No artist likes having to redo their work, so it saves some frustration! I'll explain some more, as these terms will mean very little to you right now.

The first time an artist opens a new level in the editor, it'll be a scene made by a level designer. It'll be very basic; showing how the game should work and it'll be really blocky. On all my previous games, this was the case and the first task for an artist would be to make some basic looking assets that more closely resemble the shapes seen in the concept artwork.

❑ **White box (first pass)** – The initial art assets created are known as white box artwork. This stage is a proving ground. The art assets describe form, proportion and scale and intended use, there may be the equivalent of white box VFX, lighting and animation there too. It's the first step of transforming the levels visuals.

It's an important part of the process. Some people in my experience have ignored this stage and stampede straight to the pretty final assets, but it's a costly foolish road to travel down. The goal of white box art is to prove out the game's theories, gameplay, level and visual design. It's a low risk, fast iteration process that enables the company to experiment.

- **Grey box (second pass)** – Assets progress onto the next stage of visual development, incorporating any feedback from the games review team into this next section. The grey-box asset will overall increase in fidelity, basic materials applied, additional polygons, improved animations, higher quality VFX, correct lighting, physics proxies, UVs and naming. Imagine a car in its primer coat of paint. It's all there, but it's missing the polish and final trim.

- **Final art (polish)** – This is working your grey-box asset up to its ultimate state. Everything is polished and spot on. All the assets are visually at their highest fidelity, however, when trying to get your game to run at the target frame rate, sometimes quality has to suffer and be reduced a notch or two.

- **Optimisation** – Tech artists and project engineers help to identify any assets or levels that are running slow. Every game has a target frame rate to hit so that the gaming experience is buttery smooth. When a game runs slow, it affects all sorts of things, AI, streaming, interactions, and it can turn even the best looking game into a nightmare.

  Optimising can mean simply tweaking materials to improve rendering performance, encompassing tasks like reducing polygons, bone count, or larger issues such as overdraw, draw distances, or asset count. No doubt it can feel painful at the time if the quality of your asset is lower than you would prefer, but the game must run well. It's about the big picture, not the individual asset.

- **Bug fixing** – I've yet to meet an artist who likes bug fixing. Who does? I know I'd rather be creating new work rather than fixing up art bugs, however this is another essential part of the pipeline. Every gamer can remember when they had to quit a game because they fell through the game world or got stuck in a rock because of bad collision.

  Bugs are assigned to you via your team lead and above all else, check that your fix works! Play the game and double check that it hasn't broken the game. Your lead artist will be happy forever, or at least a week.

Pre-release – Most of the hard work is complete, so now it's fixing any last determined bugs that are hanging around in the build. You won't be able to fix anything unless it's requested; the idea is to keep changes to a minimum and the game build stable.

Release – There are few times where it's calm in game development, however this is one of the rare opportunities. Of course there will be the gone-gold parties and, in that case, it'll be the opposite of calm as it's usually a free bar!

> ❏ **Downtime** – This can be the opportunity where you can brush up on your own art skills, giving yourself small projects to work on building up your knowledge base, strengthening up some areas of weakness you might have discovered in making the game and it's a time to find/read/watch anything that inspires you. Chances are you're feeling a little worn around the edges after completing the game, and you'll want to start putting back into your creative jar again.

Post-release – You might be assigned to be part of the Downloadable content team (DLC), in which case, you'll quickly start working on extra levels, usually using existing artwork or changed in simple quick ways to keep production costs down but visual output high.

So, we've gone from high-level company structure right down to what you'll face over the development of the game, and it's a lot to chew on, but it's worthwhile knowing the underlying mechanics of the company and project, even though, in day-to-day operations, you won't hear much other than first pass, second pass, final and bug fix. And I imagine if you are like me, those are the bits you'll care about most.

So, now we've got the formal structure out of the way, let's concentrate on you. We've looked at the game development system as a whole, but how does this impact your working week? How much time will you get to sit at your desk, headphones on and create amazing artwork and how much will you spend in meetings and reviews?

YOUR WEEKLY WORK LIFE

Have you just skipped right to this stage? Fair enough, I won't judge you (but I advise you to go back and read the previous chapters!). So, you want to know what your weekly workload will be? How much is dedicated to working and how much to talking? And what can you look forward to?

Naturally, how the company is set up and the production system they use affects your working life, and this varies between companies. However, it's safe to say that, as a Junior Artist, you'll experience a mixture of these five activities in your working week:

- Daily work
- Stand-ups/team catch ups
- Weekly reviews
- Feedback
- Fun

Daily work

There's a settling-in period when you first start. It's time for you to become familiar with the pipeline and art processes, during which your Lead will gauge your strengths, weaknesses, and the speed you work. Some artists are naturally fast, some are slower, but perhaps more fastidious. Everyone has their strengths and weaknesses!

Your Lead Artist works closely with the Producer, and between them they define your daily/weekly/monthly schedule. It's normally calculated in weeks and 'blocked in' on the calendar. If you are a prop artist and each hero prop takes a week to create, then you'll have four assets assigned to you for a month. It's simple, right?

Stand-ups/team catch ups

A short and informal meeting which takes place with your team. If you are in the office, you all stand in a rough circle to discuss any issues you might have and how current tasks are progressing. If you are remote working, it's a similar theme but obviously you are all on screen and no need to stand up! The idea is to catch any 'blockers' quickly, other team members can chip in with solutions and your Lead or Producer can provide the final say on how to proceed so you don't waste any time.

Weekly reviews

The focus of reviews depends on the size of the art team. If the team is small, everyone gathers in a meeting room, often on a weekly basis. Each artist takes their turn to explain what they're working on, showing images/ movies of the asset or directly in-engine. Alongside the team will be your Lead and AD, maybe even a designer. This is a great way to get immediate feedback from your seniors.

You'll find out what your boss's boss is thinking, whether you're doing the right things and if not, where to course correct. If they don't like something, don't worry, it doesn't make your work bad, it's just not what they wanted. It can be tough if you're at final art stage, thinking you are about to complete and then discover the opposite, but ideally with regular reviews, it keeps mistakes minimal and the cost to the schedule for alterations, low.

The other major benefit of having the whole talented art team in the same room at once, is that you get to see everyone's work, picking up ideas on techniques and finding inspiration, which pushes you to create more works of art yourself.

I often struggled with this in the past, being an introvert and lacking experience in my early years. If you're like me, don't worry, watch how others do it, you'll notice how they project an air of confidence in the language they use, the way they deliver the information plus how they handle questions or feedback. Having a passion and showing it through clear delivery and clear thinking goes a long way. You can learn a lot even if you tend to lurk at the back of the room.

Feedback

The game and the levels you're helping to create are regularly reviewed by the senior stakeholders, including the CEO, Creative and Senior Directors. These reviews will be less frequent and higher level, giving broad feedback to the team.

In your normal working week, you'll receive feedback via your AD and Lead as they review the content and assets during the development cycle. They'll make corrections as the project progresses, which can vary in scope. Note that you'll always get feedback, and while you might not agree with it, if they have requested something, make it happen!

I would say stay agile and 'bend with the wind' is the best methodology. The inflexible artist breaks under strain, the flexible ones make changes and bounce back when the wind has stopped blowing.

Fun: all work and all play?

Yes, fun exists; you can work and have fun. No really.

Once you've settled in, calmed down and found your flow, you'll worry less and spend more time enjoying your work life. If you're at the office, coffee breaks, water cooler moments, playing pool, hammering away on the arcade cabinets, playing basketball, foosball, video games at lunch or after work and even some after-work, social time, they are all there for the taking. If you're working from home, you can still find similar fun but in an online way, or you can focus on yourself, furthering a hobby or just simply relaxing!

 It's tempting to spend all your time learning your new craft and trying to impress your boss but also consider balancing work and life so that you start your career in a healthy way.

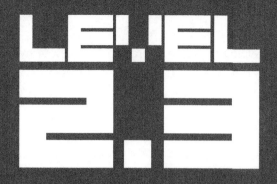

LEVEL
2.3

KEEP CALM
AND CARRY ON

HEALTHY HABITS

It's easy to think, 'Ah, I'm so young, I've got years before I need to worry about that,', but why not take the time to look after your future self, now?

Healthy habits are becoming increasingly prevalent in the games industry, and old ways of thinking, such as 'Don't take a day off when you are sick because you look weak', or 'Taking a mental health day is for the broken' are passing into gaming history. Companies are coming round to the idea that people, not machines, make their product. While you can't force people to be healthy, you can provide opportunities and reduce the hurdles to encourage them to look after themselves both physically and mentally, because the two go hand in hand.

If you think you can work a 100-hour week and come out the end unscathed, you are sadly very wrong. Reports abound of failed marriages, destroyed sleep cycles, anxiety, and weight gain from unhealthy crunch-time foods, which are so yummy and salty but so not good for you. Have I made my point? Good, because I wish someone had pulled me aside and said 'Paul, go easy, ask for help, the company isn't more important than your health'.

It's true, my wife thought I was a bit of a workaholic. That, coupled with minimal holiday allocation, questionable management practices and poor delegation, made me an overly busy guy who did little at the weekend except recuperate. Factor into that the crunch periods of over 80 hours a week, one day off a week and no physical exercise. It seemed inevitable that my body would lock up. It took a stand and said 'enough'. I couldn't turn my head, neck, or lift my left arm without massive pain, and I was off work until the painkillers, muscle relaxants and massage got me back into usable order.

That was just the physical damage, the mental damage and depression was pervasive and took much longer to get back on track. Over that period where I went to the dark side as I call it, I became a less than ideal employee while I figured out how to recharge and regain a healthy perspective.

You might think, oh, this all sounds intense and crappy, not really liking where this is going, and you would be right to think that, but only for a second.

You aren't blindly stumbling into the industry; you're reading this to get yourself all tooled up. Remember, this is about providing balance. You can't control what the games industry throws at you and how it operates, but you can control what you do to combat hard situations to bring about a favourable outcome.

It's all a balancing act. If you have a good job and an excellent manager, then life is simpler. Moral support and a healthy company culture go a long way toward improving your quality of life. I'm an artist not a doctor though (yes really!), so any issues should be discussed with your medical practitioner. Considering that, I'd still like to pinpoint some things to think about, which I consider important.

Healthy mind

The energy jar

Imagine you have a small but important jar, neatly tucked away inside you. The jar contains your creative inspiration and motivation. When you recharge yourself by doing things you love, this jar fills up, giving you the inner stores of energy and bonus brain power for your creative outpouring. When you are working hard, you're relying on those inner stores. Push too hard and for too long and your inner reserves eventually deplete and run dry.

> I'm an introvert at heart and recharge by taking time for myself. There's a lengthy list of things I enjoy, which to some would be nightmarish! These include gardening, spending time on my motorcycle, organising my garage, helping someone out (as long as it's not moving my brother-in-law's massive sofa again), small PC projects, photography, house projects, power tools, occasional socialising with close friends and family, taking in nature and walking my daft dog. These are my energy jar tasks I do to offset the stress and hopefully re-balance and centre myself.

Mindfulness

Mindfulness is a form of meditation practice. The daily practice helps deal with anxiety, create focus and ultimately move a step closer to the elusive concept of happiness. Think of this as another skill, one that over time and with practice, provides you with a clearer head, enabling you to spend more time creating rather than worrying.

> *I do between 10 and 15 minutes a day after waking up (because I like my sleep), but what counts is that I'm doing it. Health insurance providers are now giving access to mindfulness apps as part of the policy, so if that's happening, you know something is working in the campaign to improve mental health.*

Journaling

An online journal is an excellent place to jot down your daily or weekly thoughts, and the search functionality gives it the edge for me over a handwritten version. When things get you down, such as repetitive work, annoying work colleagues, repeatedly making mistakes, or loving crunch food too much, whatever it is, jot it down and get it out of your system! It's only taking up space in there, which is otherwise valuable creative space. If you notice an issue repeatedly appearing in your writing, acknowledge it, sit with it, then see if you can find a way forward to resolve it.

> *I find this works wonders, even if I can't resolve the problem, the very fact of noting it down seems to reduce its importance and weight, freeing me up to concentrate on being creative again.*

Therapy

I'm not joking about using therapy. It's more usual in the US but is becoming more accepted in the UK. Sometimes, you just don't possess the tools or the knowhow to solve the bigger issues buzzing around your head. When your washing machine breaks, do you fix it yourself or call in a professional? When your car's gearbox grinds, do you fix it yourself or call in a professional? Do you see where I'm going with this? If you have the means or can access therapy via occupational or academic provision, I highly recommend it as part of the upgrade process.

> *Practise what you preach, right? I don't mind this being in here, even if it feels highly personal. I had a long list of after-effects from my dad's death, which manifested themselves in adult life. This included behaviours that were no longer useful and were causing me more harm than good and self-protection systems that needed to change. I got there in the end. I appreciate that often money is the barrier to entry here and that healthcare providers can only offer a certain number of hours with your policy. It's not ideal, but it's a start.*

Healthy body

Exercise

Is exercise the enemy of game devs? Maybe back in the day, where lifting and drinking four pints at lunch and smoking as many cigarettes was considered exercise in some way, but not anymore. You know the mantra healthy mind, healthy body already, but are you averse to a little sweat? I was averse to all sports and competitive scenarios. My advice is to do what you can, where you can, even if that means just taking the stairs. Whatever you do, remove the barriers to getting there so that you have no excuses to avoid it.

> *I've tried all sorts, exercising with Mel B from the Spice Girls using the Xbox Connect, playing hockey for one day, trail biking, and is motorbiking considered exercise? That's maybe a stretch! I'm currently making use of the gym and since I enjoy avoiding people, I go when it's quiet in the evening. Walking the dog at a brisk pace for 30 minutes is also a great way of keeping you and your four-legged friend happy.*

Yoga

Yoga is the non-competitive stress-reducing option. A great way to give your body a good stretch, get blood flowing to your joints and boost the body and mind connection. It's also a great counterbalance to all that sitting about, and believe me, after over 20 years of making games, you'll start to feel your age if you miss out on this trendy-bendy mat-rolling water-supping slice of life.

> *I seem to slip in and out of this one, sometimes it's regular, sometimes I completely forget, I think it's the natural ebb and flow of my brain, sometimes work overrides everything else and then a week later I'm like 'hey, wasn't I doing yoga?' and start back up.*

Massage

In the UK, if you mention going for a massage, some people might look at you weirdly. To them, it's not really the done thing. If your company offers neck/back/shoulder/leg massages either free or at a reduced rate, I recommend that you book one. Stress commonly collects in these areas, and in the forearms, fingers and even your glutes.

Massage can be a little painful as your muscles are stretched and pushed into an elastic state again. For a few days after you might ache and you will probably wonder, 'Why did I do that, I almost feel worse?' But then you wake up one morning and your original pain has gone, along with your massage aches, and you feel ten times better.

> *The time my body locked up so that I couldn't turn my head or neck, massage was a huge contributor to getting me back on the road to recovery – thank you, Phyllis! As a result, I now go for a regular deep tissue massage to keep on top of work-related aches.*

Food and water

The quality of fuel you put into your body makes a big difference. At the very least, work on getting your five-a-day, and the recommended amount of water. If your company provides food and drink, but has no healthy options, ask if they will add it to the company stores.

> *Remaining regularly hydrated seems a constant struggle for me. I maybe get two to three cups of water a day and about five cups of tea with two sugars. I don't drink caffeine except for a can of Coke on a Friday as a treat, otherwise my sugar baby appears on my dad bod. The principal thing is that I'm trying. It's hard for someone with a sweet tooth!*

You're probably aware of these basics, and there's no need for me to labour the point. You'll find your own programme to achieve a healthy mind and body experience and keep yourself in good shape. Do something you'll enjoy so you have a good chance of continuing it, because it often takes 20 continuous days of a new activity for it to become a habit.

THE SIGNS OF STRESS

I know you might think, 'I've only just started, I haven't even done my first crunch yet, so there's no point talking about stress so early on!' Well, you want to be best of the best, yes? How many articles have you read about artists who were amazing, but left due to stress and never returned?

Stress comes with making games and is unavoidable with high-expectation projects. The threat of failure is all too real, and it's this that taps into the well-known 'fight, flight or freeze' response buried deep within your psyche. You want to do your best, yet there is so much to learn about both the software and the workplace.

Understanding that stress will be part of your life is part of the process; the important part is to focus on how you can identify and reduce its overall effect. We'll look at the symptoms first, then the triggers. You might ask, 'Isn't that back-to-front?' I would say no, because you'll notice the stress effect long before the primary trigger. It's with hindsight that you can react and reduce.

In the games industry, this trigger can be repetitive and possibly last for months. For example, crunch is the most stressful period with long hours and mental drain, while balancing the desire to do the best versus getting stuff done. But it doesn't have to be large and obvious as in a crunch situation. It can be smaller, involving making mistakes or not hitting expectations, or it could be project based, such as having unclear deadlines, too much work, or low team morale.

Let's take a peek at the symptoms before looking at the trigger in the next section.

The mental stuff

- ❏ Racing thoughts
- ❏ Constant worrying and rumination
- ❏ Difficulty concentrating
- ❏ Slow decision making

The physical stuff

- ❏ Headaches
- ❏ Muscle tension or pain
- ❏ Dizziness
- ❏ Sleep problems
- ❏ Feeling tired all the time
- ❏ Feeling hyper and bouncing from task to task
- ❏ Eating too much or too little

The emotional stuff

- ❏ Feeling overwhelmed
- ❏ Acting irritable and wound up
- ❏ Feeling anxious
- ❏ Reduced self-esteem

Stress can be subversive, creeping up on you slowly and getting into your mind and body, pulling levers and tugging at your strings to where suddenly you are no longer acting as yourself.

To put the above into context, if one day you find yourself irritable in meetings, focusing on the bad rather than the good, suspecting people's intentions, the green-eyed monster of jealousy rearing its head, your brain becoming so foggy that you can't focus clearly, retreating from social situations and your friends, being less flexible and responsive to change requests or seeming about to blow up with the addition of just one more small task, then yes, you are likely exhibiting signs of stress.

But what to do about it? How do you get back to normal?

MANAGING YOUR STRESS LEVELS

To get back on top, to become more yourself, look at the triggers. As a Junior, I hope that your stressful situations are in the minority. Perhaps you missed your train to work, or felt a fool when you made a mistake? You may have submitted a file which broke the game build, or forgotten to export something and a designer got all uppity with you, things like that.

If you find you are making repeated errors, stop and do some digging to find out what's going on. Please leave the self-judgement at the door. You will make mistakes, but it's how you recover that counts.

1. Ask the HOW questions:
- ❏ How am I feeling?
- ❏ How did I get to this point?

2. Then the WHAT questions:
- ❏ What don't I like about this situation?
- ❏ What level of control do I have?
- ❏ What do I do to fix the situation?

3. Then a WHO question:
- ❏ Who do I trust to help me solve this situation?

As with all introspection, try to leave your ego out of the discussion. It can be hard because that ego has helped you through some tough times, but it can also impede really identifying your issues. If you are struggling to identify the areas, peek below. You might find this list helpful in pinpointing troublesome areas that are common to the industry and which cause undue stress.

- ❏ Organisation culture (crunch culture, feature creep, wasting content and effort)

- ❏ Poor management practices (lack of planning, tasks assigned at late notice, unrealistic expectations, lack of clarity)

- ❏ Physical work environment (desk/chair/lighting/air quality/ temperature)

- ❏ Relationships at work (colleagues with conflicting personalities, bullying)

- ❏ Team morale (loss of valued staff, group negativity)

- ❏ Lack of support (not feeling listened to)

- ❏ Role conflict (unclear expectations, duplication of tasks, favouritism, undue competition)

Who can help?

If you can solve your issues directly or through a simple chat with your manager, that's great. Make the tweaks and on you go. However, if the issues are larger and involve abuse, sexism, racism, discrimination, or harassment, speak with HR first. If HR can't help you, then seek outside counsel.

 Not all HR departments are created equal! Some are excellent and value everyone equally, some side with the company and management. I'm just saying, be prepared...

IS YOUR COMPUTER TRYING TO KILL YOU?

It might feel that way sometimes, especially after spending hours on a good creative session. It doesn't have to be a crunch situation either, you could work happily away, super focused on your weekly tasks, but slowly the slouch creeps in, the head getting closer to the monitors, your eyes drying. These ailments are well documented and a genuine concern, so much so, that studios operate checks on staff and your desk environment to keep ahead of the curve.

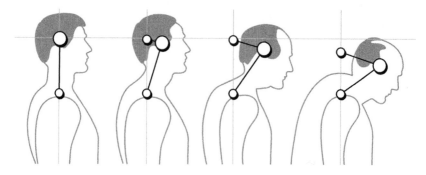

Figure 13. Computer-related posture problems

Have you noticed people around you with these body postures, the stoop, the craned neck, or the rolled shoulders like in Figure 13? While they sound like something from a kung fu Disney movie, they are very real and not just limited to veterans like me, even people with five years' experience can show early signs. You can take early measures now, which is part of paying it forward for your future self.

Let's look at the common physical ailments that can occur while your head is down and focused on creative genius, and the simple steps to keep them at bay. I'm not a medical professional though, so any worries you have should be discussed with your doctor (I feel I need to repeat this!).

Problem: Weakened core/weak back/neck. Long hours and poor posture while sitting at your workstation are the major culprits. Users often naturally 'creep' towards their monitor, but does getting closer to your pixels make them more special? I don't think so. It's a natural tendency as you get more engrossed in your work. The downside is that your body pays you back eventually with muscle pain, joint stiffness and possibly reduced blood flow to your joints and limbs, further exacerbating the situation.

Solution: Your company can assess your workstation, which involves checking seat, desk, and monitor heights. Adjustable desks are becoming more popular; ergonomic chairs and monitor risers also might help you out. Notice that I said 'help' because, even with all this equipment and checking, if you want to slouch, or sit for too long in your chair, there's nothing anyone can do. Exercising an awareness of your posture and rechecking it will help you no end.

Problem: **RSI** (Repetitive Strain Injury). A condition resulting from repetitive actions, which can affect office workers anywhere from the fingers all the way to the shoulders and neck. Symptoms often include pain, stiffness, tingling, numbness or cramps.

Solution: In an ideal world, prevention is better than cure. Simple checks on your posture and workstation are preventative acts, as are alternating between mouse and pen, taking breaks, stretching exercises for your aching limbs, and regular deep tissue massage to stretch those tendons and improve flexibility.

Problem: **Eye strain**. Those pesky pixels give your eyes a battering, making them flit around, examining and checking, processing, tweaking and squinting. It's a full-time job. Pain, dryness, or blurred vision are common issues, with headaches and migraine being the top ailments.

Solution:

a) Check your seating position, do you sit under an air conditioner? AC diffusers can help alter the airflow, though often the best solution is to move desks.
b) Check you have adequate light fixtures and light levels. Glare from poorly shielded lights can trigger headaches. Improving your surrounding light levels (eg from a desk lamp) can help too, reducing the glare and contrast from your bright monitor and dim surroundings.
c) Is your monitor too bright? Reduce the level or switch to a low contrast user interface on the software you use.
d) Be sure to take regular eye tests and schedule breaks. Like the rest of your body, they need looking after.

Problem: **Diet**. We've looked at lighting and seating, but what about the food nasties stacked in the company larder? You'll find high-salt snacks, high-caffeine and sugary drinks, biscuits, and odd things with a half-life of a thousand years. In your twenties, you may think your body can take it, but unless you take care of your body, you'll take on the shape of an old potato. Garbage in and garbage out.

Solution: You know this already, right? Use the best fuel you can to keep you in top shape; a healthy body makes a healthy mind and vice versa. Keep track of the food you take in, limiting those sugary treats and greasy pizzas. Drink water and limit caffeine, although green tea is the exception with its reported health benefits.

Most of this is straightforward stuff, but it's also simple to ignore and let fall by the wayside. I certainly don't expect you to be perfect, but you can make small tweaks over time and build it up. Like going to the gym, you don't hit the top weight straight away; you build up to it, then you can see progress and feel the benefits.

NO TO NEGATIVE BEHAVIOUR

As an artist, you're now part of the creative gang that forms a large part of the games industry, one which is still young, still learning and still making mistakes. On starting your new job, guided by this book, you'll help make the industry a better one, more tolerant, more accepting and more inclusive.

This is all sounding idealist, isn't it? But why not? Why should you put up with unacceptable behaviour and poor standards in an industry just because you are new? It's hard if any of these issues happen to you, I suffered bullying early in my career and it took a while for me to even accept it was going on. Once I did though, I could address it and get back on top.

Some examples of unacceptable behaviour are:

- ❏ Aggressive or abusive behaviour, such as shouting or personal insults

- ❏ Spreading malicious rumours or gossip

- ❏ Discrimination on grounds of race, gender, age, body type or religion

- ❏ Sexual or any type of harassment

- ❏ Unwanted physical contact

- ❏ Stalking

- ❏ Offensive comments, jokes, or gestures

- ❏ Publishing, circulating, or displaying pornographic, racist, sexually suggestive or otherwise offensive material or pictures

- ❏ Isolation, deliberate exclusion and/or non co-operation at work

- ❏ Persistent and unreasonable criticism

- ❏ Unreasonable demands and impossible targets

- ❏ Coercion, such as pressure to subscribe to a particular political or religious belief

The reality is that all this still exists in organisations. When people feel powerless, this stuff continues. Thankfully, more and more people are stepping forward, taking massively brave steps to highlight the injustices that have occurred.

If you experience anything on, or like, this list, speak to HR first, to give the organisation the opportunity to right the wrong. If you find they aren't listening, then look for outside counsel.

COMPANY SOCIALS

What's not to like? Free food: check; free alcohol: check! Living the dream now! You are working for a kick-ass company, making great-looking assets, and now part of a strong art team. When a company party is announced, it's time to let off some steam, kick back, drink a few mai tais, chug some beer, sneak in a cheeky tequila shot; what could go wrong? I think you know where this is heading.

Party on!

Not everyone loves a party but, for those who do, you'll have more than your fair chance at your new company to let your hair down and enjoy a bit of social time with existing friends and maybe even make some new ones. I'm not your parent here, and everyone has overdone their alcohol intake at some point I think it's fair to say. Go easy, because even at a company party, you represent yourself and the company. If you go too far, you'll find out the hard way.

Real examples of going too far at company parties

- ❏ Broken ankles from jumping off balconies

- ❏ Parts of body flesh missing (owner can't remember how)

- ❏ Sexual harassment, grabbing body parts over and over

- ❏ Throwing up all over the staff coats in the cloakroom

- ❏ Harassing the boss's partner

- ❏ Swapping clothes with the party host

- ❏ Standing in the hotel foyer in your underpants

- ❏ Damaging company or event property

Drunken behaviour isn't always funny

What might be funny to you at the time might be hugely offensive to others. Watch out for making the mistake of ingesting alcohol but no food, or you'll be in real trouble. Before long you'll hit that sweet spot of buzzing and then fly right past with a long visit to the porcelain portal.

Some of the examples listed above are more serious than others, and some will cause a visit to HR or worse, the police.

Want to get fired?

Although the event may have a free bar, it's not a license to lose self-control. The consequences can be swift, and you could be cautioned, fired or end up in front of a judge in court.

> *I feel I must also balance this section out because I've had far more good times than bad by a ratio of about 10:1. Sure, it's fun to have a drink and relax to celebrate team achievements, but if you want to go wild (whatever your definition of wild is) I suggest you do it in your own time with real friends and not at the company event.*

The company social is one upside you'll experience as part of working in gaming. That's the social side covered, but the next section looks at the welfare and financial sides. Some of these are not really given the limelight that they need, especially when considering future you.

LEVEL
2.4

SHOW ME
THE GOODIES

PERKS

I used to take these for granted. Maybe I've become more Zen, or just more thankful for the small things in life, who knows, but really, who doesn't like free stuff? I think half my wardrobe is game company gear and at one point I had loads of gaming memorabilia. After another moment of Zen, however, I sold most of it (which I slightly regret) but the fact remains, companies are savvy to you (and me) liking treats in whatever form they come. The goodies are getting better and better as companies vie to keep your attention and loyalty. The list below includes some commonly experienced perks:

- **Swag** – Free T-shirts, hoodies, hats, scarves, statues, 3D prints, desk items that light up or game completion items as special edition trophies/objects that you can mount on a wall. The list is endless.

- **Free food/drinks** – Some places have canteens with free or subsidised food, pantries full of candy and free drinks, fruit, nuts, coffee, and tea or even an in-house barista.

- **Flexible hours** – Need to run to the shops or drop your dog at doggy day-care, don't want to be fighting with traffic? Shifting your hours about can help with that.

- **Working from home** – Avoid the long commute, just work from home. The benefits are massive, more time with your family and friends. The downside can be a degree of loneliness and possible lack of team cohesion.

- **Maternity/paternity leave** – Important time off for new mums and dads. Best to do your homework on this, time off allowance and whether it's paid for varies.

- **Subsidised gym** – Often memberships are expensive, so the company will contribute a good percentage of the monthly fee, keeping you healthy and not breaking the bank account.

- **Employee referral bonus** – If you get your friend a job and they successfully make it past the probation period, companies will pay you a bonus. Get another friend in, you win again. I'm not talking life-changing money, but it'll pay for a game console.

- **Company events** – Gone-gold parties, summer BBQ, holiday season get togethers, often free bar and free food and entertainment.

- **Wellness programme** – Activities to promote good health, flu shots, meditation, weight loss, smoking cessation, health screening, etc.

As you can see, there's a mass of offers to keep employees happy. While some people may value them more than their salary, it's important to understand the wider context of corporate benefits. Similarly, company benefits are the big brother to the little perks. Incentives and bonus schemes can make a big difference to your life now and in the future if you take them seriously. I find all these benefits are really types of investment, in both your health and your finances, so let's take a deeper look at the rewards you can reap.

BONUS INCENTIVES

This is what you want to know really, isn't it? Headline-grabbing, large pay-outs are the stuff legends are made of. Tales abound of employees making it big and retiring, or buying a house or new car with a bonus. To be frank, who wouldn't want a bit of extra cash in their bank account? The lure of the bonus is strong, and if you work for a company with high rewards, there will be high demands, the two go together. If you're not careful, you could chase the promise of a bonus at the cost of everything else.

In my career, I've been lucky to share in the success of multiple companies. Was it right time, right place? Probably. In my second game job I joined a new company and had the chance to buy stock in the venture, so I invested £8,000 of my own money, which was the last of my inheritance. It was a risky move, but I knew some of the team and the CEO was my old boss, so I felt it was a 'safe' bet. Initially, I made some money, which paid for a new kitchen in a tiny house my wife and I had bought. As the company expanded and became more successful, my shares grew and so did the value.

When I came to leave the company, they gave me some poor advice. It was from trusted sources and being young and naïve; I took their word for it. I left the UK and went to work in the US. In this time my old company was bought out, and the value of my shares was initially strong. By my calculation the shares were worth about £350,000. I didn't sell my shares on the advice they gave me and two years later, the company folded (it's a long, complicated story). By then, my shares were worth the gut-wrenching sum of zero pounds. A hard lesson to learn at any age.

My move to the US turned out to be a good one though as Epic Games was about to create another winner. They had the Unreal Tournament series and games engine, but they were making an alternative universe and game with a next-gen version of the Unreal engine. Gears of War turned out to be a knock-it-out-of-the-park winner, and the bonuses were sizeable. For some it meant life-changing amounts.

Talking to others about this, it seems I got really lucky. But opportunities exist, especially if you're the sort to take a risk, but it's not something I'd advocate without doing your homework and having a fallback. Remember, this is the exception rather than the rule. As a new player in the games industry, your options are normally limited, especially if you are joining a well-established company. But don't let this put you off! Bonuses do happen (when companies are successful), maybe not life-changing amounts, but smaller and more frequent, and my philosophy is that any extra that turns up in the bank account is always appreciated.

So, let's look at the common ways employees can be rewarded:

- **Personal performance bonus.** As part of your regular Personal Development Review (PDR), you'll be assessed on performance (we cover this area in depth later), and how you perform will influence your bonus rating. How each company calculates its score differs, and in some you accumulate points, while elsewhere it's a number assessed and given each year.

  This is normally a yearly bonus which is an extra sum of money around the end of December or near the end of the tax year. This only happens when the company can afford it. No money in the bank, no bonus. It's discretionary, so try to avoid falling into the trap of expecting a bonus.

- **Project performance bonus.** Say that the game you have worked on for years sells millions of units and the company makes large amounts of profit. Some of this profit will be assigned to a bonus pool. Your contribution to the project, time served, bonus tier (yes, there can be different multipliers) and your previous personal performance reviews influence how much bonus money you receive.

- **Share options.** While less useful to you now, it's worth being aware of your options further on in your career. These are sweeteners to attract and keep senior employees. What's the big deal about becoming a shareholder, you might ask? It's another way of gaining more money on top of everything else! Here are some essentials of share ownership:
  - You can hold stock in different ways and companies offer different tiers of ownership.
  - An option, as it's known, allows you to buy shares, at a pre-approved price, off the company at a later date. When you purchase your share(s), they call this exercising your option.
  - Options are not real shares until they are exercised. Therefore, while you have these options, all you have is the right to buy shares in the company in the future.

- The Incentive Stock Option (ISO) is the most common of stock option schemes, but as I mentioned, there are others that can be offered by the company.

- **That's all good, but how does it benefit me?** By having shares in the company, you can make more money in other ways:
  - If the company does well, it pays bonus money to the shareholders, which is called a 'dividend'. So, you, as an employee, potentially, can get a bonus on a bonus on a bonus.
  - If you decide to sell your shares in the future and the value of each share has gone up, then you will make a profit, adding more money into your account. Conversely, if you sell it when the value has dipped, you will incur a loss.
  - All this extra cash will be taxed. Remember that nothing is free!

Things to think about

- **Invest in yourself.** Don't blow what you earn on things that lose value, and instead buy things that are an investment (health, skills, knowledge) and use it to level yourself up.

- **The golden handcuffs.** It's possible to get to a point in your later career where you hate your job and love the money. You stay because of the high salary and/or bonuses each year, but you are desperately unhappy. It's a well-known situation, and it's important to sit down and really figure out what's going to make you happy. It might involve less money, only you will know what to do!

- **Financial planning.** The secret to good financial health is good financial planning. As discussed in the pension advice section, find a good financial advisor, but don't blindly leave it in their hands. I recommend you keep up with your own regular financial planning. After all, it's your money, so don't you want to know where it's going? Don't be frightened of what seems a complicated area. If you take control, you'll find it liberating!

PENSION SCHEMES

If I said that you could enter a scheme in which, if you paid in £100, someone gave you another £100 on top, would you be interested? And if you could do that every month, year on year, would you be interested? Then if in 50 years, you could* have access to just under half a million pounds, would you be interested? Of course, you would. So, let's talk about pensions!

*It's all theoretical at this point. Investing £200 a month for 50 years with a 2.5% yearly interest rate and at 3% inflation (cost of living) would generate £463,736.11.

Stick with me because I think it's important. This section is all about future proofing yourself. It's the 'plan today, live well tomorrow' school of thought, no sticking your head in the sand! Just like I'm not a doctor, I'm also not a financial advisor, so seek professional advice when the times comes.

Here are some common questions on the subject:

What's a pension?

In basic terms, when you're working, a pension is money put into an account, which you do until you retire. Some of this money comes from your salary, and, if you work for a company, some is paid in by your employer. On retiring, you get to spend that money, and if your investment has done well, you'll have enough for an enjoyable old age.

Why start as early as possible?

The earlier you start, the better off you will be in the future, especially if your company offers to match the amount you put away each month. That's doubling your money right there.

Aren't pensions risky?

Pensions are investments, spread over company stocks, shares, cash and property to name a few. Investments can go up in value and they can go down. When you take on a pension, its risk level is derived normally from your attitude towards risk versus reward. Your pension advisor will help with choosing the risk level that best suits your current circumstances. Pensions are not a short-term gamble, they're part of a long-term investment strategy.

Where can I get more advice?

You can find independent financial advice or, as is often the case, the pension company will provide financial advice as part of the pension package they create for your company. Pension companies have websites to view and track your investment.

I've heard many an artist profess they have yet to log in, so please do so at least once a year to keep track. That way, when you have your yearly review with the financial advisor, you'll be better prepared to ask questions. Don't worry, this isn't an exam and stupid questions are always welcome, otherwise, how would you learn anything?

Ok, sermon over. In short, get investing in yourself and therefore, your future.

INSURANCE

While not as immediately interesting as bonuses and saving for your future, insurance is there to provide stability and security for you as you develop your career and is therefore just as important. It's more important than ever that employers provide an attractive package as part of the benefits to tempt you away from any competitors and keep you within the organisation.

I think we've established that your health is important to you and to your new employer, so let's look at some common insurance schemes made available to staff:

- ❑ Medical insurance (mental and physical)

- ❑ Dental insurance (keep those choppers clean)

- ❏ Vision care (eye checks)

- ❏ Critical illness cover (when you can't work, covers your costs depending on policy)

- ❏ Death in service (normally two to four times your annual salary)

People pick their companies not only for the projects but also the benefits they offer, which applies especially to artists in the US, where there is no national health system.

Health providers have become increasingly savvy, including rewards with their health plans. You can now earn goodies, such as free cinema tickets, coffees, reduced price gym equipment and footwear, spa breaks, etc all based on how much you exercise. They will even subsidise the payments on personal health-tracking devices, so it is well worth doing those extra steps every day to reap the benefits.

Because of the complexity and variety within companies, I advise you doing further homework doing further homework before starting with a company and understanding their benefit systems. It's all too easy as a Junior Artist to sign on the dotted line and think 'I'll worry about that another day,' but with a little extra digging, you'll give yourself a stronger foundation.

LEVEL TWO SUMMARY

That's quite the download! But it's how you'll get ahead of the others, and by having this knowledge ahead of time, you will be much better prepared and in a stronger position to achieve what you want.

Your early years really set you up to leap up the ladder, but before you leap, walk. Let's see what lessons you remember. If you missed something, that's ok, just go back and re-read what you need.

2.1 Gear up

- ❏ Understand what's in store as a Junior Artist.
- ❏ Did you read Amber's account of her time as a Junior? It's interesting stuff!
- ❏ It's a marathon, not a sprint, so learn who's who, and what's what.
- ❏ Contracts might bore the pants off you, but they are important to understand. Avoid the IP trap.
- ❏ Get to know your Human Resources department, you might need them one day.

2.2 Onwards and upwards

- ❏ Aim to pass your probation the first time, it's important to your progression.
- ❏ Take the time to settle in when you first start, read up and do your homework.
- ❏ Knowing the company structure helps understand how the company works.
- ❏ Art teams can be set up differently depending on the game, company, and time frame.
- ❏ Tasks come from the top, but it's not a simple journey.
- ❏ From start to finish, from concept to gold, we spread shipping games over six stages.
- ❏ By the time you ship your first asset, it will have been through many iterations and reviews.

❑ Weekly life is a heady mix of making art, reviews, team meetings, and maybe even some fun.

2.3 Keep calm and carry on

❑ Health is important, consider it from the outset, not after or during the hard times.
❑ Be mindful of your surroundings, how and where you sit affects your performance.
❑ Keep on top of stress; work out the cause and how to reduce it.
❑ Identify areas that cause you hardship at work; spend time to really find a way forward.
❑ Be professional, no one wants to see you in HR's office for a stupid mistake.
❑ Have fun at company socials, avoid stunts or words that could be career limiting.

2.4 Show me the goodies

❑ Who doesn't like a perk?
❑ You can make more money from bonus incentives; shares are always a good option.
❑ Get that pension rolling, set yourself up for the future.
❑ Having protection is the smart move, make the most of company insurance schemes.

That's your introduction to life as a Junior Artist!

You should now have a good understanding of the foundations of the company which you're helping to support. You also know what's expected of you, your daily life, and things to look out for that could be problems if you take your eye off the prize.

An artist normally has this junior role from one to two years, depending on the project. In the process you'll build your skills both in artwork and confidence and learn the ropes, but at the back of your mind, you know, there's a bigger slope to climb. Thoughts of stepping up start bubbling up, and you'll soon ask yourself how to get onto the next rung of the career ladder.

How do I become a Mid-level Artist?

I'm glad you asked, because we are about to move on, to look at how you cross over, the obstacles in your way and when you cross, what you'll find waiting.

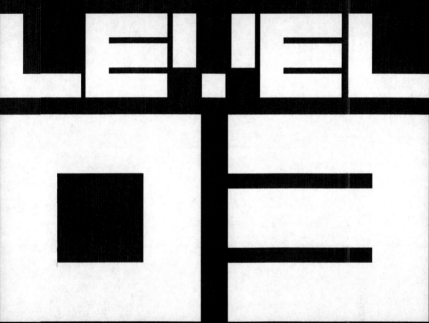

POWERING UP!

After a year, you might find yourself thinking, 'What's next? How do I climb higher? I want more responsibility!'

This is great! You need an insatiable curiosity and a desire to keep moving and progressing, because if you aren't moving forward, then what are you doing? Many an artist has lost their way in the later sections of this journey; either a misstep has taken them off the ledge, or they got lost in the blizzard of discontent and burn-out. These next chapters explain how to progress safely, to cross over from Junior to Mid-level Artist, then Senior to the Principal Artist role.

Now it's time to find out which skills are needed for you to level up, why they're needed and what happens if you don't acquire them.

These skills and strategies form the backbone of your personal development. These are the glory years, a time where your hard work can really pay off, but you already know what's involved! Dedication, graft, and the desire to advance, and that's just the start of the leveling up game.

Instead of you trying to guess the rest and learn the hard way, let me give you a helping hand. Read on!

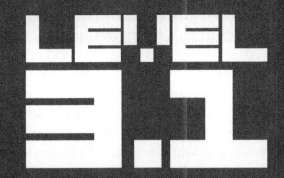

LEVEL 3.1

BIGGER,
BADDER
AND BETTER

UNDERSTANDING THE THREE ROLES

Let's address the elephant in the room. Yes, I've listed four roles because it made sense to roll it back a bit to give you the full context. You already know what it takes to be a Junior and, after reading this, you'll know what defines the three up-and-coming roles you can advance to before deciding where you want your career to take you in the future.

- **Junior Artist:** Needs oversight for basic tasks (covered in Level Two)
  - Initial stage of discovery, learning pipelines and art processes.

- **Mid-level Artist:** Needs oversight for more advanced tasks
  - Growing artistic skill sets, working with others on more challenging assets.

- **Senior Artist:** Needs little oversight for advanced tasks
  - Well-developed artist, capable of delivering solutions in a timely manner, mentoring others, shows strong art and technical skills.

- **Principal Artist:** Needs minimal oversight for complex tasks
  - Top of the artistic career path, pushing boundaries for the Art Director and setting standards for the art team.

At each stage of your development, new skills are acquired and bolstered, starting with artwork, software, and techniques. They build over time, to where you can create complex assets or levels, collaborating with more departments, co-ordinating and mentoring. Ultimately, if the studio has the position, you could reach Principal Artist, with the option of doing everything yourself or with a small strike team.

The beauty of these roles is that they involve your development. No official management duties are required, no giving reviews, no granting or denying holidays, no wondering why you are in so many planning meetings; it's all artwork and personal development. However, you'll want to keep in the back of your mind that communication is critical. It's as much the key to advancing as your pen and tablet. Let's break this down a little more for each aspect and look at what's involved.

UNLOCK YOUR MID-LEVEL ARTIST

The Mid-level Artist is a bit like the middle child, the Junior gets a lot of attention, as does the Senior, but with added responsibilities piled on top. But the Mid-level Artist can often go a little ignored even though they are the foot soldiers building the game in return for a reasonable wage.

The role is a stepping stone; you gain skills and confidence, but what you really want is to become a Senior (not all companies have Principal Artists). Seniors get the juicy stuff. The work is more complex and rewarding, plus it looks great in your portfolio. I liken it to the teenage years of your career.

You're growing in all sorts of areas. No one really knows which way you'll go, but how you handle your development will shape how quickly you'll be promoted. Like those teenage years, you can't avoid nor fast track them; you just have to go through it.

Advancing from Junior to Mid means that you're expected to already be able to deliver a finished asset, something relatively straightforward and which you can integrate into the game build without problems. You'll understand your department's pipeline and how to hit your deadlines while delivering a quality simple asset.

Moving up to Mid-level Artist means being expected to handle more advanced assets, with more responsibility and greater autonomy. By comparison, in the junior role you may have been building simple props or scenery assets for example. Now you'll be taking more on, maybe building out an environment with a Senior Artist, or taking established pieces and building more assets to increase the modular set, while applying existing style guides to maintain a cohesive look and feel.

But don't just take my word for it. To illustrate, I've interviewed a Mid-level Artist for his impressions of the role.

SLICE OF LIFE – MID-LEVEL ARTIST INSIGHT

Let me introduce a talented artist on the rise, one who's battled his way up the ranks from Quality Assurance (QA) and now is making waves, pushing his skills, climbing that mountain. This interview is a great insider's look into the nuts and bolts of artistic life in the games industry.

Q. Who are you, what is your job, how long have you held this position and how many years' total experience do you have?

A. My name is Luan Vetoreti, I'm currently [at the time of the interview] a Senior Environment Artist at Cloud Imperium Games (CIG) and have been for a couple of months now. Previously, I was Mid-level for just over two-and-a-half years, and before that, I was a Junior for about a year-and-a-half. I have about five years' experience in the industry, having done some freelance, a little bit of QA, and having started my environment art career at CIG in 2016.

Q. Why did you choose to work in games? What was the attraction?

A. There wasn't a single thing that led me to choose a career in games. But I can pinpoint the moment I started thinking about games as something I'd like to somehow work in back to when I first played *Baldur's Gate* on my dad's PC. In a lot of ways, even now as an environment artist, I'm kind of fulfilling the storytelling aspect of that spark I had as a kid.

Back then I was super interested in writing stories for games. As time passed my interests shifted to music, which I did pursue professionally, and even did some music for a couple of commercials, and I wanted to do everything I could to write music for games. Halo was heavily responsible for my love of using music as a way to help tell stories. But as with anything in life, things rarely go as planned. I knew I wanted to somehow tell stories for games, the only thing was trying to find the medium that was going to help me achieve that.

As the career in music died down and the time came to go to university, I was enamoured with *Mass Effect* and its absolutely wonderful environments, so that's when I decided to do a course at the Norwich University of the Arts in Games Art, where, after a lot of different ways of doing art, I settled on environment art. But throughout all the different things I've been exploring to get into games, the one constant was telling stories, in whatever way I could.

Q. How did you find the jump from Junior Artist to Mid-level? Was there a jump or was it a smooth transition?

A. For me it was a very smooth transition. I'm quite ambitious and very proactive, so as the months passed as a Junior, I took more and more tasks on myself, and explored more and more ways of doing things better and more efficiently for the team. I've always enjoyed trying to make the team work better, be it by making texturing tools, standardising workflows, or even just taking some time to teach someone something. Due to that I've slowly gotten more and more responsibility as the months passed. By the time of the promotion (both to Mid-level, and Senior), I was already doing the tasks that that level required of me. So, it was fairly seamless all things considered.

Q. Do you have a routine to get you into work mode?

A. I think I am the kind of person that really takes a little while to engage the full creative mode. So, whilst I don't have a specific routine, I usually have to start my morning with a quick browse of ArtStation whilst drinking a coffee to get inspired, and maybe throw in a podcast to get my brain thinking about things. Then it's just a matter of starting my tasks in a manner that progressively gets me into the full swing of things.

This usually consists of doing some simple design challenges by working on a small part of the environment, or some nice mindless and fun modelling like mapping texture trims to an asset, and then starting to solve bigger parts of the environment I'm working on from there. I find if I just open up a location as the first thing I do in the morning it usually makes me stare at it blankly for quite a while without solving anything.

Q. Has anything taken you by surprise in the role? Types of tasks or expectations that you weren't aware of?

A. When I started out, some of the optimisation techniques that are standard but unheard of outside of studios themselves really took me by surprise. Like having to design spaces in ways that the player doesn't see everything at once or doesn't have insanely large lines of sight.

Back then I found that kind of stuff incredibly limiting, but, as time passed, I learned to turn that in favour of the things I work on. Be it by making simpler meshes with quieter designs that are more appealing, or spaces that have interesting transitional areas so that you don't have a million things on screen at once, but the environment flows nicely. Those are things that I still learn more and more to this day, but luckily we're at a time in the industry where the power of current and next-gen technology makes it so that I can achieve the look I want fairly effortlessly, with just a few mindful decisions about where to cut some corners.

The other aspect that really took me aback was how much I was expected to design my own spaces. As my roles have evolved, I have worked with less and less concept art, to the point where the concepts I get are few and far between, and instead I just work really closely with the Art Director to establish the look of a location.

Before I got into the industry, I thought my role would almost entirely be to just make things that are given to me based on a concept image. The fact that I've had to do so much of this myself in my four-plus years at Cloud Imperium has made me quite proficient in designing things much like a concept designer would, which I'm very grateful for!

Q. Have there been areas of the role that you have struggled with? What were they and how did you overcome them?

A. Some of the technical aspects when it came to the rendering side of things took me a long time to even begin to understand. How long things take in terms of "milliseconds" to render and ways to make that better is something I'm always seeking to learn more about because I've always struggled with the logic side of things. Math has never been a strong suit of mine (I am an artist after all!), so ways of optimising a shader or even the cost of lights that cast shadow in an environment were things I never once considered before I actually joined a real studio production. Often when talking to a rendering engineer I need to pick apart what they're saying bit by bit to make my brain catch up to it, whereas some of my colleagues tend to understand those kinds of challenges pretty well.

Ultimately the way that I manage to stay on top of these things is really by just learning about it in my own time, studying it like I would for a test in school. That way, the next time I talk about how a specific aspect of the tech is expensive I can engage in the conversation and help provide solutions.

Q. Have you experienced any crunch yet and what techniques do you employ to combat the stress?

A. Luckily not really! There have been a few weekends where I've worked due to getting something ready for release. But mostly any overtime I do is out of my own volition. I strongly believe that overtime should only ever be a choice of the employee, and it represents a fault in scheduling. I just make sure my tasks are always done on time. If I need more time on something, I try my best to minimise how much extra time is needed.

Q. What has been the defining moment of your career so far?

A. I had the chance of being one of two artists responsible for making an entire planet covered by city and manmade objects. To this day I've never seen anything quite like it in any video game, and I enjoyed tackling all the crazy challenges that the task presented. Being able to say I made an entire planet covered by city is quite something!

Q. Some say that the Mid-level Artist is the forgotten artist. Do you feel that?

A. I can understand why some people think that way, after all the Senior has so much responsibility, and so many students get highlighted as they begin their career and their jump to a Junior Artist, that it's easy to forget that there's a whole host of Mid-level Artists in a production. So, the spotlights are on the fresh, or the fully levelled up.

That said, the Mid-level Artist tends to be the biggest workhorse for the production. Whilst the Senior is busy with managing their environments or setting standards, and the Junior is getting some of the simpler and easier tasks, the Mid-levels are pushing out content after content. Even within the team it's easy to mistake the attention that the Senior Artist will get for being so busy and running things, and all the attention the Juniors get because they're hungry for knowledge, for the Mid-level being forgotten. But it's more that the Mid-level is autonomous and can make their own decisions, so they'll happily produce content away in their corner.

Q. What do you think becoming a Senior Artist will grant you?

The biggest thing for a Senior in my opinion is a chance to set real standards, not just in the quality of the work, but also in how to communicate with other people and departments. It's so important to make sure that you're providing a smooth experience for the rest of the team. I really like making sure that the team is empowered, and that any issues they have can be resolved as easily as possible, and having that extra responsibility given to me with the role allows me to make sure that these things happen, as I can have more impact in the running of the department.

Q. Making artwork all day for a job is hard work, right? How do you maintain your creative passion, do you do more artwork or do other things to balance out your life? (No judgement here!)

A. It's not something that is easy to do. I am always super excited to work on my personal art, I get all these great ideas throughout the day, think of things I want to improve on or change in a piece I'm working on. But when it gets to the end of the workday, I just can't bring myself to open anything and start any kind of creative work. There're a few ways I deal with this, however. The first is not to pressure myself into having to do any personal art. If I do this, it makes it feel like work. I just take it slow, and if all I manage to do that week is push a couple of verts to the left, then so be it, I'll get there eventually, as long as I have a clear goal of where I need to get to.

Another thing is to make sure I'm giving the people I know and love enough time and attention. Be it by relaxing with some friends and playing games, or spending time with my girlfriend. I spent a lot of my life focusing on work and work only, and the only way to make sure that I'm not drained from work nowadays is to make sure I get that social interaction.

And ultimately, I just reward myself. If I've made some nice progress on a piece, and I'm aching to play a game or watch a TV show, I do. Whilst I always make sure I do some art throughout the week outside of work, I very much enjoy just doing what I want to do, when I want to do it. A lot of people would feel guilty for doing something else instead of honing their skills, and I get it, I feel it a bit too, but I know that I'll get to it, and the refreshed mindset will help me create things I don't dislike.

Q. If you could snap your fingers and make yourself an expert in one area of game art, what would it be?

A. For me specifically I'd love to be an expert in designing environments. Not necessarily concept art as is, but being able to take something underdeveloped, and work out everything from shape language, to how the world affects the design of the location, to the lighting. I suppose that is akin to art direction. But if I had to pick a more specific area, it'd probably have to be lighting. You can do so much with good lighting; you can take incredibly simple assets and make it feel like something so much more than it is. It's easy for environment artists to forget lighting, and focus on texturing, or modelling, but lighting is what brings everything to life, so it's something I think I'd love to master.

Q. If you had something to say to your Junior past self, what advice would you give?

A. Be more open minded and less frustrated with some aspects of game development. Really just be more patient with everyone in general. It was easy for me before to just get annoyed with something that gets cut, or some tool that doesn't work, or someone who's doing something wrong, and just annoy people by being somewhat short or blunt. It took me a little while to adjust how I deal with these things, so I wish I could've gotten to this point sooner. It's something I'd probably recommend to anyone, instead of complaining and getting annoyed, try to solve the issue, talk to people and just don't get frustrated. You'll end up making things better for everyone.

Luan Vetoreti
https://www.artstation.com/illusivepixel
https://www.exp-points.com/

BECOMING SENIOR ARTIST

The coveted Senior Artist role is a bit like a prize fighter in that, when you win this, you know you've really earned it.

To achieve the title, you'll have a few (game) titles under your belt, having steadily worked your way up. Your art skills have progressed to a point that you know you can tackle almost anything thrown at you. Your work ethic is strong, you know you can step up in times of stress or when the chips are down, and the project needs a final shove to get it done. Once you get the title, you're at the start of this role, but by the end you'll be a fully seasoned pro.

You form a pivotal part of an art team. For your Lead Artist, you are the go-to person, independent, self-supporting, trustworthy, and yet still able to take advice and direction. A good Senior is worth their weight in gold.

A Senior Artist is also someone who can mentor. You aid the development of Mid-level Artists and Juniors, and can work with new recruits and settle them in. Wisdom learnt in the trenches with techniques and pipelines is passed on regardless of missing documentation. You help set the standard of professionalism in all areas. The load can be heavy, but people management is minimal and informal, providing you with the time to carry on making artwork.

In terms of that artwork, your workload is more significant. Because of your knowledge, you're able to take assets from concept to reality. Your work often includes the juicy portfolio quality stuff. On top of this, you'll help advance the look of the game by providing high quality work for the key stages of production. This might include models, shaders, rigging, VFX or level set-up, among others. It can be wide and varied!

> *After being a Lead at Epic, I returned to the role of Senior Artist at Rocksteady Studios. Going from a charged management position to a content creator felt good. I found it refreshing to build something that I could say was mine, as well as focusing on pure artwork and polishing my art skills. Looking back, I remember the challenge of making Batman: Arkham City fondly, even though it was a shock to the system to be in the trenches again, I'm still proud of the work created on the underground train station, sewers and the Wonder Tower. I would have stayed longer if London had stolen my heart, but Manchester was calling, and my landlord was booting us out.*

The Senior Artist has the luxury of staying at this point almost indefinitely. Often, Senior Artist is the last 'pure' art job title (if the Principal role doesn't exist at the company), and for many it's a safe place, the culmination of years of dedication. Like I did, you can choose to go up and down, from Senior to Lead to Senior, so nothing is set in stone.

Senior is a varied role, with plenty to keep you interested. Don't believe me? Read this next slice of life from Ryan, a veteran Senior Artist in the industry.

SLICE OF LIFE – SENIOR ARTIST INSIGHT

A heavy-hitting role, and where artists really start to flex their wings.
Find out directly from Ryan as you read his account of how he's grown over the years, honing and sharpening not only his art skills, but planning, mentoring and time management too.

Q. Who are you, how long have you held this position and how many years' experience do you have?

A. I'm Ryan Howard, I've held a senior role in the games industry for the last 9 years, and in total have 14 years' experience.

Q. Can you describe your experience of being a Senior Artist thus far?

A. It has a lot of ups and downs and comes with a lot of responsibility. But there is a lot of satisfaction seeing the finished project and knowing how much you contributed to it. Overall, I've loved it, and seeing Juniors you have trained straight out of education step into high-level positions as their career progresses is incredibly motivational.

Q. Who are the people you regularly collaborate with in your week to week (departments or people)?

A. Art Director, Design, Production, Cod/Tech Art and other members within the art team from Principal to Junior.

Q. Like a seasoned artist, you have experienced multiple roles and returned to the position of Senior Artist – why was that?

A. There is always room in the art field for experienced Seniors. There are very few jobs above this role due to the pyramid structures companies tend to follow. Having multiple voices at the top can be very distracting when the team needs clear direction and leadership, but passing some of that responsibility down to the Senior level who are also experienced not only lightens the load for the Lead/Directors, it empowers the team and gets better work out of them. The key is hiring experienced Seniors who may have held higher roles elsewhere. I was told something at the beginning of my career, that said you might be their boss right now, but your next job they could be your boss. I have experienced that very thing. Roles chop and change across the industry and studios/jobs come and go, it's just part of the job.

Q. What would you say defines a Senior Artist? Is it experience, length served, agility (feel free to add/subtract)?

A. It's a combination of things, but length served definitely has an initial say. You have to have experienced the highs and lows of a few development cycles/public releases to learn the ropes, but after 3-5 years, when you have gone through this, it comes down to knowing the ins and outs of production, and being able to adapt on the job when things come from left of field. Likewise, the obvious strong technical understanding of art pipelines and a high expectation and delivery of the quality of art are a must.

Q. What changed when you were promoted from Mid-level Artist to Senior?

A. Responsibility and my own expectations of myself, from the teams I was part of, and what management expected of me. Ownership of areas/levels became far more important and being able to schedule for yourself and others and manage a small team were all new experiences that were learnt on the job.

Q. What separates a Mid-level Artist from a Senior Artist?

A. Practical and technical experience, planning and management skills are the difference between a very strong Mid-level Artist and a Senior, it really separates the two roles. Seeing issues before they occur, even when they are just on paper and drawing on your experience to prevent those issues arising again are huge requirements when becoming a Senior. Being able to train lower-level staff and pass that knowledge on also is hugely required in this role, and done right, it can really let those Juniors become valued members of the team.

You are no longer building an asset in isolation, or making some really cool shader in Designer, you are expected to deliver that as standard. You are trusted to help steer a small portion of the team and project to get all of its parts over the line. It's a big step up from only worrying about yourself and the task you have been given.

Q. Crunch is a dirty word at the moment with many devs voicing their unhappiness; what are your thoughts on crunch and work-life balance?

A. This is a topic where I could write a book on my feelings.

There are two key things that spring to mind when I think of crunch:

1. It's unavoidable in the way game studios are run, but it is manageable when done right.

2. It is very easy for crunch to leave a bad taste and cause burn-out when there is no end in sight or for giving over your own time with little reward.

Work-life balance is essential to avoiding burn-out, you need to be able to step away from the work and clear your head. There must be downtime if you want to remain creative and hungry. So, uninstall Teams/Scratch/Outlook from your phone or turn it off and step away, otherwise you will burn out.

My view on crunch has changed over the years. When I was young without a family, I did the crazy 100+ hour weeks, but it isn't sustainable and leads directly to burn-out. I don't look back at those times fondly, outside of the great people I worked with. Thankfully and unusually, I was paid overtime and that isn't standard when on a salary. My own inexperience caused the hours I worked at the time but many a time a project has been too big or too badly planned to deliver a complete product that will hit a release without it.

From a project point of view, crunch shows poorly managed decisions and a failure in the process, be it from the publisher side (marketing feature creep or shifting or aggressive milestones), or the developer side with bad management of a project, having a poor pipeline, feature creep or an inexperienced team over-extending themselves.

Crunch inevitably happens at the end of a project, and with an end in sight like going from Beta to a Gold Master (GM) release date you can at least cope knowing it will end, but when you are crunching from pre-production onwards, then maybe the scope and scale is something that the studio wasn't set up to do and the learning on the job could have been better utilised. It's an ugly word for a reason and I hope our industry can mature to avoid it [happening] more regularly.

Q. Would you consider taking a Principal Artist role if it were offered?

A. I have, but from what I've witnessed you can become a bit of a lone wolf in this role. I like working directly with a team and I've lent more to the Lead side of things than the Principal Artist. I'm always up for a challenge so it is certainly something I'd go for if I fit.

Q. At fourteen years, you have some titles on that belt, what keeps you going? Often this can be a time for artists to plateau, what motivates you to keep on pushing?

A. I love the industry and I love games. Seeing artists dropping bombs on ArtStation and playing awesome games always makes me want to step up even if I sometimes feel wrongfooted by seeing something amazing. You have got to be hungry to keep in the job, otherwise you just won't make it.

Q. Who's more important – Lead Artist or Art Director (kind of a trick question)?

A. There is a role for both. I always see the Lead as more of the manager and the Art Director as the visionary. Both need to play off one another as ying to the other's yang, otherwise things can lean too much into the art, or too much into the numbers and technical stuff. It's a balance and a good team of Lead and AD will get that and work together to build good products on schedule that look great.

Q. How would you describe your working style, and have you found a type of personality that may cause you to reconsider how you approach a problem?

A. I'm fairly laidback most of the time, but I work very hard day to day. I think my personality allows me to fit into most teams but certainly everyone can improve and learn from each experience they have and grow to be better.

Q. Have you any regrets in your career? We all do, right? What did you learn from them?

A. Honestly everything happens for a reason, good and bad. I don't regret anything as every decision has brought me to where I'm at. There have been times where I could have gone to big AAA studios/incredibly large successful games and worked on some classics and part of me wishes I did, but being a tiny cog in an enormous machine isn't always what it's cracked up to be. That option is always there if you continue to push yourself, so I don't regret not taking some of those opportunities as they will come again.

Q. Some say the Senior Artist role is the best one, what do you think of that?

A. As a team member it's certainly the best. You aren't the proper boss so can still be one of the gang, be part of the social, have a laugh and you aren't the grumpy boss. But you still garner the respect of the team when you need it. It's a nice feeling from a social point of view, and from a work point of view you have the ability and skills to own a part of the game without the pressure from roles above this position. It certainly has its perks.

Q. If you had any words of wisdom to pass down the ranks, what would they be? Think hard, because this is going to be immortalised!

A. You can't know everything. Be humble, accept help and learn from those around you regardless of their seniority/experience. Never stop learning as the tools and techniques change every other year and you will get left behind if you don't keep on the edge of the newest and best, but don't forget your basics. Share your knowledge with those around you and bring everyone up together, you are only as good as the team around you. There is no place in the games industry for a lone wolf, it's a team job and you need to be agile and open to others' input to build the best thing you can in the time you have. Work hard so you can play hard.

Ryan Howard
https://www.linkedin.com/in/ryan-howard-30a3a59/

THE PRINCIPAL ARTIST

The Principal Artist is the pinnacle of the game artist's career, in the sense that it is the top of the art pool, often commanding high status. The best part of the role is not being distracted by management meetings, team reviews and micro-management, they might not even have a team if they don't want one. It's not always a role available in companies but is becoming increasingly common as a career path for artists not wanting to head into management.

Principals can often be the lone wolf, developing pipelines and new artwork, working hand in hand with an Art Director (AD), and the graphics and design directors to propel the game studio forward, way before the rest of the team. Think of them as a scout, out ahead finding issues, pushing the boundaries, helping to develop the look and feel and achieve the Art Director's vision, bringing back new information and skills required to develop the main art team.

On the flip side, a Principal can operate a small crack squad, an advance group developing a new look for the new IP. New techniques can take years to integrate into an existing pipeline, so this squad helps the transition from dream to reality.

As a Principal you are expected to work with the AD to help develop the vision. It can be a tag team if done right, with each person pushing the vision along and improving the product. This work will help define the next generation of game artwork. The Principal takes the AD's vision, namely the concept art, and nurtures it to life in the game engine, assets, lighting, shaders, animation, scripting and cameras, to craft an advance experience for the senior creatives to review. Time spent here can save countless hours of work further down the pipeline.

You might be asking why, if the role is so good, doesn't everyone have this position in their company? Put simply, not everyone feels they need one but, as we've established, it's one of the next steps for those who want to remain on the creative career path, providing creative freedom and higher salaries.

SLICE OF LIFE – PRINCIPAL ARTIST INSIGHT

Even less information is available about Principal Artists than all the other roles. I've had to pull all the strings and do some hard super sleuthing to bring you someone that is well worth the title. Though in the past he has had the title of Expert rather than Principal, we figured it's the same, bar the name. Introducing Chris Wells.

Q. Chris, tell us a little about your current role and how long you've been in the industry.

A. My current role is Lead Character Artist at MountainTop Studios, a remote start-up working on a competitive shooter. It's an honour to work with truly exceptional people coming from different areas of both games and tech industries. I've been in the games industry for 22 years; does time ever fly.

Q. Ok, let's get back on track. Expert Artist, what constitutes being an expert in your mind? 10,000 hours, true grit, a drive to be the best?

A. For me, it's always been about being open to learning, improving your skills, and loving the pressure of making something new. The pursuit to improve and grow as an artist never really ends, but it's the pursuit that keeps things fresh.

Q. How would you describe your working week as a Principal? Were you a one-man army or part of a strike team?

A. In my experience the strike team is critical, because if you have the right people the free exchange of ideas/brainstorming produce a much better result than if we go it alone, at least in the initial phase. Once the rough plan is sorted out, however, I think heads-down time is necessary to really focus on the goal. It's a tricky balance, in my opinion: too little collaboration can produce a disjointed result, and too much leaves little time for refinement.

Q. I imagine there's a lot of pressure with this role, would you say that's true? Do you experience nagging doubts like the rest of us and how in the past have you dealt with them?

A. There's absolutely a lot of pressure, but that pressure can bring out the best in people. There's a lot of fun in figuring out a new visual style/feature for a game. You just have to have an attitude that it's ok if the first try doesn't land well, it's just part of the process and have faith in you and your colleagues will get there eventually and it will be that much more rewarding.

Q. To be a Principal, you must be top of your game. What techniques or routines keep you in tip top shape and motivated, both body and mind?

A. Principal Artists in my experience tend to have a restless spirit and a desire to grow. They tend to have an independent streak and enjoy the process of creating the best work they can. There's a book I read from every once in a while, when I feel burnt out and need inspiration: The Art Spirit by Robert Henri. He was a fantastic artist and teacher in the early 20th century and really encouraged his students to do great work and not be discouraged with creating their own style, because this will inevitably come if you put yourself in your work where you can.

Q. What would you say have been your top moments in your career? Any lows to match, that you care to share?

A. For me, the top moment in my career would have to be working on the Gears of War initial trilogy. It was an incredible team of people we had, who were very down to earth. The style of the game, with its melancholy atmosphere, macho heroes, and army of seemingly insurmountable monsters really dialled into what I loved my entire life. As for lows, I would say the closing of Boss Key Productions was the most disappointing moment in my career. Before joining a start-up, it's important to recognise the risk of failure, which I did, however, on paper it felt like we had the right pieces to make it work. That said, I learned a lot from the experience. It's always important to keep a desire to grow, remember that we all want the project to work, and never to rest on the achievements of the past because it can limit your willingness to approach a problem in a new way.

Q. Like me, you've travelled about for your career, what advantages do you think that's afforded you?

A. Travelling is something that's had a profound effect on my life and my work. It makes a person more open minded if you're in a learning frame of mind. I could associate these places I visited with the friends I made along the way, and not just a spot on a map or article I read. In my career it's really helped because it's much easier to connect with people abroad professionally and to have patience when trying to communicate ideas, because I've been in similar situations abroad where I wasn't able to communicate because I didn't know the language. In short, travelling makes it easier to put yourself in someone else's shoes, even if there are things in their way of life you would do differently.

Q. Our industry seems to be in the wind of change, are there things you'd like to see more of, to progress us past our teenage corporate state?

A. Times have changed for sure. Art asset creation has a much more streamlined, assembly line approach now, which is a natural progression, I think. The scale of AAA projects these days is such that lessons learned from the film industry are increasingly employed in game studios and are necessary to survive and lean more towards making safer established IPs. On the other hand, you have a lot of small indie studios who occasionally strike gold with a megahit, seemingly from out of nowhere, again similar to the current state of the film industry with a breakout romance comedy or drama coming from a studio with limited resources, but a fresh idea. I'd like to see more medium-sized studios find success because I love the sweet spot between the wonderful innovations and team large enough to provide refinement and enough content to enjoy.

Q. I ask everyone this, looking back, what advice would you give to little Chris Wells, something that you wish you'd known before you set down the current path?

A. To little Chris Wells I'd say continue to grow and be willing to learn lessons along the way, however tough they may be. Passion for the craft is a great thing but remember that everyone on your team is a human being, and they have feelings and most have a passion for what they do as well. Soft skills are just as important as artistic talent, so treat the art of diplomacy with the same respect as your craft as an artist.

Q. And finally, what wise words would you give to someone wanting to become an Expert/Principal Artist?

A. To someone who aspires to be a Principal or Expert Artist, remember to keep the drive of always working to be better and love the challenge of that. The ride never ends until it ends.

Chris Wells
https://www.artstation.com/chriswells

I think it's fair to say, there are a good cross-section of answers here, ranging from the relatively new artist to the ultra-experienced, spanning countries and budgets. If there's one thing that's common across all titles, it's commitment to your craft. To rise through the ranks, you'll be looking to get promoted once you've learnt and polished your skills, which brings me neatly (as if I almost planned it!) to the art of the promotion!

LEVEL
3.2

LEVELLING UP

GET PROMOTED

The simplest way to climb the ladder and take yourself one step closer to the peak, is to get yourself promoted! But what's the best way to get promoted? Obviously, your artwork is one area, and the other is your level of professionalism, or the way you operate with your teammates and other departments. But how is this all measured; how do you know if you're doing well?

Over a year your performance and development will be tracked, encompassing the highs and lows, conduct, artwork, precision, decision making, time keeping, asset tracking and whether you take too many coffee breaks. If your boss misses some things, their friends and team no doubt will pick them up.

Your company will use an employee review system, which is both for you and your company. Armed with the information collated about you, your boss can accurately assess your performance. Of course, you want to know where you are doing well (pats on the back are always welcome) but also the areas where you can improve. It's a chance to discuss bothersome issues or situations with your Lead and really get a good idea of your development.

Either your Lead Artist or Art Director (AD) will conduct the review (or both), but chances are, until this point you've had little chance to sit down with them and discuss things that matter to you; they'll have been super busy. Via reviews, you'll have at least one opportunity a year, maybe even two, to have a face-to-face chat.

- ❏ **The yearly review** – This is the formal one, where performance, salaries, promotions, and bonuses are decided, all the important stuff.

- ❏ **The mid-term review** – This is the 'may, or may not happen' review, where you discuss progress six months into the role (see also the probation section of Level Two). Some companies choose not to as it takes extra time for the managers and HR department. It's more of an informal check-in.

As I mentioned, your Lead/AD has the task of collating information, sifting, comparing, and categorising against the company's vision of good or bad. The best part is, regardless of where you go, what country or company, everyone is looking for the ideal employee so the categories are very similar (usual caveat – everyone does things slightly differently!):

1. Communication and teamwork
2. Quality and creativity
3. Knowledge and skills
4. Commitment and reliability
5. Productivity

Each section of the Personal Development Review (PDR) is evaluated. Both you and your manager fill in the review form to record both sides of the evaluation story. The process goes something like this:

- For each category, you can self-grade or comment on yourself depending on the system.

- Your manager takes your comments and information into account and writes their own thoughts on your performance. They might have information from other staff, which contributes to forming an accurate picture.

- You meet to discuss what you've both written.

- Based on the conversation, you'll be given a performance assessment.

- The five sections are graded based on company guidelines.

- Grades might be A-E, 1-5, or strongly agree all the way to strongly disagree.

- Your manager submits the form to HR, where it's reviewed again and stored in the company's system.

The grading sadly isn't a universal system, and different companies operate different methods. The system appears to be wholly subjective, and while some managers will mark hard and low, others you'll find mark high and easy, which obviously can give some artists an unfair advantage. But not all is lost!

As a final check for fairness, HR and studio managers review the PDRs for consistency. They'll be on the lookout for managers marking too hard or for no good reason. Part of the balancing process is to take the final numbers/rankings and make them fair and consistent across the team/studio.

> Some companies operate a 360° review feedback system, whereby your boss reviews you, you review your boss, and your team and colleagues also have input. Don't be naive like young Paul Jones was. Your comments are not anonymous, the reviewer (your boss) can tell from the language used, the issues raised and the overall style of your review. Don't go hell for leather writing about how your manager is completely useless and should not be in charge of people. It only gets you into trouble!

 There are ways of saying what you think and still being professional. It's part of developing your soft skills.

Now you know the basic framework of the PDR, let's dive deeper and look at what's involved in each of the categories. With this, you'll have an inside track on what your company looks for and how you can improve your own skillset ahead of review time.

COMMUNICATION AND TEAMWORK

The first of our five categories sounds straightforward enough, but what do these words mean in the workplace? When it comes to your review what will you be judged on? If you're to succeed, you need to know what kind of situations arise and how to deal with them.

I'm only scratching the surface here, so to delve deeper, I would highly recommend reading books dedicated to the subject. But I'll try and break this down into what matters day to day.

At work, there are different modes of communication. As you climb the ladder, you'll be more and more visible; your company will want more from you and you'll want to consider altering the style and content of your communications. You might already be tailoring your content and not even be aware of it.

Communication types

Your working life is going to require a mix of verbal and written communication, and depending on your personality, it'll veer more one way or the other. I'm an introvert who has learned some extravert skills, but my natural tendency is towards the written word. However, I know I need to keep communications up with my team, and face to face is much stronger for building relationships in the workplace.

- **Written** – Emails and chat software are everywhere. They are part of the environment and are highly useful, being quick, simple, expressive (you can tack on an emoji), and immediate (you can get the answer you need quickly). The downside is that the tone of emails can get lost, because people can interpret content differently.

- **Verbal** – Face-to-face communication is always going to win when it comes to making connections and solving difficult issues, especially delicate or personal ones. Video calling has become ever more important in a world of distributed workflows, and while it is not as good as being there in person, it has massive advantages. When it comes to global events, even with reduced costs (no travel needed), you can work with talent from all over the world. It also provides greater flexibility for recruitment if you are happy to work this way.

Types of communicators

As you gain experience, you'll notice more and more how people interact, how they communicate and, most importantly, how their style affects you and vice versa.

> As an inexperienced artist, I remember blundering my way through, I was who I was, said what I would normally say, didn't temper it to the person or the situation. I was the introverted bull in the china shop. I'd like to think of myself as assertive these days, but sometimes the old ways try to creep back in. Everyone is a work in progress.

Above I mentioned assertiveness. Of the four types, that's the favoured personal style within most organisations and my preferred option. There are another three that go alongside it, and we'll look at them in turn now and how they operate.

- ❏ **Assertive** – Clear and direct, with no disrespect to others. Assertiveness is often confused with aggression because you're asking for what you want and being your own advocate. However, as an assertive communicator, you are also open to discussion or compromise and you value other people's needs as well as your own. To be assertive does not mean your way is the only way. Your tone and how you say or give feedback is just as important as the content. You deal in facts and not generality or exaggeration.

- ❏ **Aggressive** – Your needs take priority over others with a no compromise and no regard for the other person. This can often be 'My way is right; your way is wrong'. As an aggressive communicator, you can often be defensive or hostile, lacking empathy for other solutions and dominating the situation. Your view on things is correct, everyone else is stupid. You may resort to the blame game, criticising rather than looking for the underlying problems and offering open solutions.

❑ **Passive** – The opposite of assertive. You won't push your own ideas forward, rather you'll follow someone else's. Decisions are deferred to others, you have trouble expressing your feelings and needs, which can lead anger to build up, creating tension, and you actively avoid confrontation. It can leave a person vulnerable to abuse in the workplace through bullying, overwork and being the digital donkey, meaning they carry the majority of the load rather than it being shared, or they only get the menial parts of the game pipeline to work on.

❑ **Passive Aggressive** – A mixture of passive and aggressive. You give with one hand and take with the other. You appear calm on the surface, but it is masking hidden aggressiveness, while anger builds under the surface. You appear helpful but often leave others feeling undermined, confused, or resentful while you do nothing to help the situation and can actively make it worse behind the scenes.

These communication styles are like flavours, you might be spicy, bitter, mild or a bit of everything. Your communication style affects the people around you, you're part of a team remember? Your Lead or AD will be looking for specific qualities. Let's do a quick round of questions and answers to quantify what your reviewer might be judging you on.

What is good communication?

As a Junior, good communication could look something like this; you ask pertinent questions and listen to the answers, making notes to avoid having to ask the same questions later. When you have a problem you try to find a solution before asking, and this way you are better informed. You let your Lead know if there are any problems and don't leave it to the last minute. You click 'yes' to meeting invites so organisers know who is coming. You can explain your workings in team reviews, clearly and concisely, and you don't waffle on. You don't pretend to know everything.

As you rise through the ranks, communication skills and nuance get more important. Your involvement with other departments will be greater, so being able to communicate ideas, thinking, priorities, levels of risk and becoming a solution provider are paramount to getting ahead. Naturally, this will be delivered in an assertive manner and without being manipulative.

There are people in the organisation who will test you, unknowingly, and part of your journey is to figure out how to work with them. You might not like a person, but you don't have to be unprofessional; they might have good information but are spiky or poor at delivering it. You'll need to take the nuggets of information and let them carry on, unless you are their manager of course, in which case you'll want to address their issues to foster a better working environment.

What is good teamwork?

In an industry that attracts introverts, teamwork can be a foreign concept initially. People like to hunker down, headphones on, and sit in their bubbles. Being a strong artist does not automatically make you a team player. Going back to the Everest analogy in section 2.1, you don't get to the top on your own, you'll need a support system.

A good team player is someone who works well with others. They can work on their own, but also provide support, by listening or helping others with problems and offering solutions. This isn't a do it all day, every day, kind of thing, it's a when the occasion requires it. We all have our own schedules and deadlines to hit anyway. If a problem is too big, you might suggest that artist takes it higher up, to a Senior or their Lead, it's important you don't take it on. Another facet of a good team player might include owning up to a mistake you have made, and not throwing one of your team 'under the bus'. Be the grease, not the grit, to your Lead. As a professional artist you help solve problems, not create them, either overtly or behind the scenes by complaining and moaning in the break room.

As a team player you contribute to building a trusting environment, where peers know they can trust you with tasks, help and feedback. You help them up when they are down and celebrate the small wins as much as the large ones, which people often lose sight of. A simple thank you for any task goes a long way, especially in this industry where large portions of work can be taken for granted.

Everyone needs to let off steam, it's natural, but even on a Friday night at the bar, if you find yourself part of the crowd complaining and undermining other staff, stop and think about what you are doing, because by doing this you are contributing to a negative culture. Problems are not solved this way, so look for ways to improve the situation actively and in an assertive manner. Be the grease not the grit!

QUALITY AND CREATIVITY

Next up are the areas you care most about, the driving force of any artist. Creation! To build something out of nothing and craft away until the asset shines; that's the quality aspect. Creativity and quality share a happy little home in an artist's head, it's what makes you get up in the morning, switch on the PC and get crafting, day in, day out.

Without this dynamic duo (quality and creativity), game designers could still make a game, but I'm 99% sure it would look dull and uninspiring (sorry designers!)

So, assuming you bring your A game each day, when it comes to review time and you are judged on quality and creativity, what's the metric? Can it be quantified, or is it subjective and all in the eye of the reviewer? Plus, what happens when you don't feel the love and feel a need to jump start your artistic self?

How high is high when it comes to quality?

For a Junior's role, the quality bar is set lower. But as you rise through the ranks, you'll have years of knowledge and experience to fall back on, so even if stuff does go wrong, you know in the back of your mind that you can pull it all together. You only get to the Principal role by being a leader in your field.

- **Experience** – There's only one way to gain experience, or as my old colleague Texas Pete used to say, 'log the hours'. There's no escape; do the work and push through the barrier of making mistakes. When you're learning new software or skills, making mistakes feels less painful, as it's offset by the good feelings of achievement and creating something fresh.

- **Time** – To craft a quality asset you need time, and if you don't have time, you need a toolbox of shortcuts at the ready. As your experience grows, so will your toolkit, enabling you to spend less time wondering about process and dedicate more time to creativity and delivering high quality work.

- **Skills** – Initially, it's about an asset moving through its pipeline. Your Lead will be evaluating progress, noting whether it's a smooth or bumpy transition. Did lots of things go wrong, did it take twice as long as expected, how did you cope with the challenges? In terms of artwork, you'll be judged on your skill in taking an image and converting it to 3D, to following direction, maintaining the artistic vision, scale, proportion, form, visual balance, contrast, colour, material definition, shader construction and usability (does the asset work for the game, for design and art?).

- **Tenacity** – Determination is what you need, and bags of it. You'll hit problems, perhaps with the game tech, the engine, naming conventions, rigging errors, collision meshes, designers being unhappy with something, colours too saturated, style not quite correct, texture too large, UV islands inefficient, I could go on, but what would be the point? It's all about finding a way to fix the issue, and if you can't, find help, then fix it.

Fostering creativity

At every position on the artistic career ladder, there's opportunity for creativity, and the higher you go, the greater the opportunity for creative freedom.

I'm not talking about going rogue and making artwork that doesn't work for the game. The higher you go, naturally the more experienced you'll be. Your head will be full of ideas and techniques and ways to improve your own art, and you create inspirational artwork with little assistance. Roles such as the Senior and Principal Artist, for example, have the skills to take what they know and really push the thinking forward, complementing the Art Director's vision.

When it comes to the all-important review time, these skills, along with artwork and decision making will be evaluated. Figure 14 has been adapted to describe your journey and development in our industry (original source Peter Nilsson, 2011. https://drive.google.com/file/d/1lH9wkpvBkW-bNOkzpBVX15EvpWcKohmK/view).

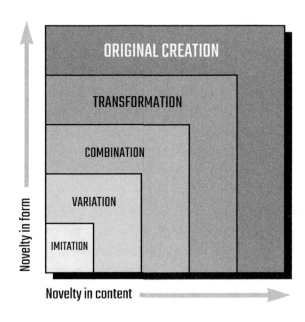

Figure 14. Development of the creative skillset

Junior Artist – Imitation. At this stage of your career, all your effort is devoted to learning the pipeline and content creation methods. There is less emphasis on creating something new, and more on duplicating and replicating. Can you create assets in the prescribed style? Can you get an asset through the pipeline and into the game without errors?

Mid-level Artist – Variation/Combination. Based on your pipeline knowledge and the art style, you're able to take ideas (maybe just verbal, no concept art) and create variations on a theme. Building on the confidence gained in your first year, you are hungry for more and ready for bigger challenges. With guidance from your Lead and AD you can deliver full assets that help expand and develop the game.

Senior Artist – Combination/Transformation/Original Creation. Stepping into the world of original creation, you'll have a broad and deep skillset, meaning you can take whatever you're given and build it out from the ground up if need be. You have the confidence and art knowledge to take that scrappy, loose single sketch you were given and turn it into a full level, character group, or band of crazy zombies each with unique weapons, and it runs at the target frame rate.

Principal Artist – Original Creation. You take all the above and roll it into one. You can create something from nothing with the confidence that it'll look amazing. The Principal helps drive the Art Director's vision based on a chat and a few images for reference. You can help bind the artwork to the design and deliver an early experience for the player, develop new art techniques and pipeline alterations for future game engine development, or advance tool sets to make the art team's life easier. Fewer complications for the team equals more artwork and faster iteration.

Your Lead will be looking at all these areas. While not normally defined, or at least, I've yet to see a company lay it out in black and white like this, these are the notes that they'll mentally be looking to measure you against, to see how you are developing.

 Be open to learning, from whomever is willing to offer up hints and tips and tricks, young or old, junior or senior, designer or artist, because everyone has experience from which you can benefit.

KNOWLEDGE AND SKILLS

Your knowledge and skills are vital to levelling up, that's a no brainer, right? Most artists focus on artwork, which makes sense, as it's more tangible and if you don't know something, I bet you can find a tutorial on it. These would be 'hard skills'. On the opposing end is something wrigglier and harder to get your arms around (for some), namely the soft skills. If you want to rise through the ranks, you'll need bags of both.

Hard skills

These aren't things that are hard to learn, most are easily teachable and measurable. Think of what you have on your resume, the courses you've taken, the classes finished, the software learnt and to what level. The games industry requires a huge number of hard skills that require your attention. How you gather, learn and the speed at which you develop them will directly affect your rise through the company.

At the start of your career, this is about learning the pipeline. As you progress, focus shifts to pushing content through the pipeline faster and more efficiently. It's just as important to diagnose how to fix a broken asset as it is how to make something from scratch.

Skills are easily measurable by a Lead Artist. Over time, they'll see how you shape up using new software, creating assets with or without assistance, evaluating if you're prone to mistakes or able to improvise, how accurate your work is technically, how close to the art and design brief are you, or whether you make good choices in your art fundamentals. These are all hard skills.

Soft skills

Juniors and Mids are often preoccupied with the hard skills. But soft skills are the opposite of hard skills, they're subjective. You might know them as interpersonal skills. We've already covered communication, which is the biggest of the soft skills, but others include teamwork, flexibility, motivation, collaboration, problem solving, empathy, positivity, open mindedness, and emotional intelligence.

It would be a mistake to assume that the older or more experienced the artist, the better their soft skills. The danger for some can be a lack of awareness that their soft skills aren't as strong as the industry requires. A seasoned effective Lead Artist or AD will be able to spot these habits and direct them towards something more positive.

To climb that ladder and reach the peak, you need just as many soft as hard skills. When you reach management level, it will all be about negotiation. After all, who are you negotiating with? People. People like you.

COMMITMENT AND RELIABILITY

No, this isn't some sort of wedding vow. Your company does want artists who are committed to the cause, turning up day after day, reliably pumping out artwork and getting the game made. But it's never just that straightforward, is it?

To be promoted you want to be the person who can deliver, hitting deadlines and providing quality assets. Put simply, are you trustworthy?

- ❏ **Time keeping** – Do you arrive on time and work your hours? Do you go the extra mile when asked or when just a few extra minutes can save the rest of the team hours?

- ❏ **Office attitude** – Are you a helper or a hinderer? Do you give and take, or just take?

- ❏ **Assets** – Are you hitting the quality mark and on time, is your work accurate?

- ❏ **Integrity** – When you say you'll do something, do you and is it of the required quality? Are you aware of the impact on your team if you don't get the work completed?

❏ **Agility** – How flexible are you, can you swap onto different tasks or do you require a more linear flow of work?

❏ **Communication** – Do you communicate clearly and ahead of time? Being pro-active when the unforeseen happens is much better than hoping to the end that 'it'll all work out'.

❏ **Peers** – Do your peers see you as reliable, are they working with you or against you?

❏ **Estimates** – How well do you estimate tasks, scope, scale and time?

As you gain rank, these factors remain but the stakes get higher, your tasks become more complex and multi-threaded as you work with more departments. The knock-ons of your decisions are greater because of the greater number of people they touch.

 When it comes to estimating the time for creating an asset, it's best to add some extra, to account for any errors or problems (they always happen). Don't over inflate but do give yourself a buffer, because it'll reduce your stress and make you more effective.

PRODUCTIVITY

It's fair to say that everyone wants to be productive. But as the saying goes, being busy doesn't necessarily mean you're productive. So, if you aren't measured by the mouse click or tap of the pen, what does your manager look for?

First, let's consider what makes one person more productive than another. To answer that we need to ask another question, ie what is productivity? Productivity is a way to measure efficiency. If you are efficient at what you do, you are getting results by achieving your goals in less time and with less effort.

For an artist, a single asset is composed of a hundred smaller tasks, each one dependent on the other, so a mistake early on has repercussions. While it might be fixed, that comes at a cost of more work, time and money. While it sounds bad, this is natural at the start of any creative process, especially in games.

As we've covered before, making artwork is half creative and half technical problem solving. Let's look at some areas I think form some of the building blocks of a productive day.

Motivation – This massively influences how productive someone is. An artist engaged with a project can overcome huge hurdles if they've fully bought into the project. For this to happen, normally someone must be happy with the art, the leadership, the company and, not only that, see a future and are committed to building it one asset at a time. They feel appreciated and their effort is recognised. They feel good about themselves and their team and, put simply, love their job.

Time – Some artists (ahem, me sometimes), like to put in extra hours. If you like your job, you can't help it, you're doing what you love, so why not push a little harder to see what you can squeeze out of your day; just one more asset, one more tweak. But as you know, I don't recommend burning out, it's better to make your day productive by focusing, working smart and then going home on time. Balance is key, you want to be keeping that internal creative bonus jar topped up by doing things other than work.

Experience – Experience plays a large part in how much work you can deliver. The Senior and Principal Artists are the heavy lifters of the team. Junior and Mid-level Artists are still building their pipeline knowledge and figuring out how they like to work, learning the best processes, discovering which actions cause mistakes and which make their lives easier. Sadly, unlike the *Matrix* movie, you can't just download the info; it's about building on your successes.

Support – If you feel supported, you feel recognised and that your work is valued. You're far more likely to be motivated. Artists can fall into box-ticking mode when they aren't motivated; work might get done but it won't be their best, providing lacklustre assets.

Planning – If you're someone who plans your work in advance, you'll come out on top in the end. It can be tempting to stampede in and 'get making stuff' but it's better to pause, plan and then execute, having noted tricky areas in advance. Doing your homework means that the final execution will be quicker and smoother.

Multi-tasking – It's official! People can't multi-task or context switch as some call it. Hopping between chats and image browsing, or Netflix and assets, takes its toll. Every time you switch, you lose your momentum and break your line of enquiry. It's best to keep focused in blocks of time (45 minutes) and then take a short break. You aren't a machine; there'll be periods where you're more effective and some when you slow down. It's natural, so go with the flow and make the most of your up time.

Boundaries – It's ok to say no, but as an artist, you need to know how. A simple tactic is to say 'Sorry, I'm in the middle of something right now, can I get back to you later?' This defines your boundary as you might be unable to interrupt your artistic flow. Doing this won't offend the person asking, but if they look like they might crumble without help, you can still decide to break off and assist them.

Ok, that's five for five. I hope this has given you an insight into what you'll be judged on by your Lead Artist and Art Director. While I imagine it feels overwhelming trying to digest this, my advice would be not to try. This isn't a test; you'll do what comes naturally at first and only then will you start to notice the gaps in your skillset. From then on, it's a process of plugging them (sometimes over years). Some of mine are like a leaky bathroom seal, occasionally failing under high pressure, but I'm not going to beat myself up, I'll just keep plugging away, like you.

We covered the five categories for a reason, an important one. To climb that ladder, you want to get promoted. To get a step closer to it (more normal), you'll want to have a good review from your direct manager. Known as the PDR (Personal Development Review), you'll get the lowdown on your progress, where you've done well and which gaps need filling.

THE PDR MEETING – ARTIST EDITION

We'll cover this from the point of view of the artist being reviewed (the reviewee) by a manager (the reviewer). Later in the Lead Artist PDR chapter we'll look at the process of holding a review and what to plan for.

A PDR, delivered well by a good manager, can be a thing of beauty. Both parties emerge beaming, and you feel buoyed by the recognition of your work and progress. Your manager has a warm fuzzy feeling, knowing they've made someone's day just a little bit brighter, because there's nothing like delivering good news.

Prior to your PDR, ideally throughout the year you'd have had some mini feedback sessions; do this, change that, that's good, nice job, all things that indicate how you have progressed. In an ideal world, you'll enter the review and there'll be no surprises.

You could see the 'but' coming, couldn't you?

Unfortunately, we aren't in an ideal world and, as you already know, the games industry is one big work in progress. I gave you a glimpse of a good review right at the start, and it's easy to imagine, isn't it? You can feel the warm glow from a good review and no dings on your record.

But what happens when you underperform? Worse, you had no idea and you're sucker punched. If, like me, you didn't see it coming, it can cause feelings of anger, confusion, or embarrassment. It can be hard to step back and see a way forward. What follows are some reasons I think this happens and what to do about it.

Flawed process

Managers, especially new ones, can shy away from tricky or sensitive issues. Even some seasoned managers will brush them off and hope that the problem magically solves itself, which 99% of the time, it won't. There are managers that are so busy that they won't prioritise reviews over their other tasks (again avoiding the problem), while others won't even notice because their own managers don't know how to properly manage staff and so it trickles down. Managing people effectively is a whole separate skill.

Minor improvements

The little ding, even if it comes out of nowhere, is harmless. Typically, something will feature on your PDR report as an area to improve upon, like time keeping, create better UV islands, improve shader network, check your work before submitting to the build machine, provide a cleaner layout of Photoshop layers. That kind of thing, all natural and part and parcel of learning your craft and improving in the industry.

Major improvements

For whatever reason, you may end up in a review session and receive feedback on your performance that you didn't expect or see coming. It's rare, but it does happen.

Ideally, your manager would have spotted it earlier and brought you in for an informal chat, to soften the blow and come up with ways to improve the situation. How your manager addresses the issues and your relationship with them will have a big impact on the outcome. But the fact you've had a heads-up is good; you'll have time to try and start to resolve the issue before the formal review.

> *At the time this happened to me it felt very out of the blue. I also found it very confusing, I was being rewarded for over delivering content and quality but being punished for poor team communication. In hindsight I can see why it would happen, I had retreated into my comfort zone and concentrated on what I could control. Communication didn't come naturally to me and I didn't know what was expected for the Lead role, no one had ever sat me down and said, this is what we expect.*

It's natural to feel hurt, aggrieved or angry, and want to challenge your reviewer's opinion, or become demotivated. But regardless of who you are, there are ways of helping yourself no matter how bad you feel or what emotions are being triggered.

- Absorb the blow. Maybe you didn't see the problem (obviously you didn't, you would have fixed it if you had!), but your manager has seen it and brought it to your attention. At the time, you can ask for more clarification, but not all of us are level-headed and clear thinking at times of stress, so listen away, take notes and know that you'll be coming back to this at a later date.

- After your meeting, spend some time reflecting on what happened. Try to figure out what's being said. If you can't understand it, that's ok, it means that you don't know what's being asked of you and therefore you need more information. You can't solve a problem unless you fully understand it. If you want to vent (try and get this over with quickly as it will hold you back from the problem-solving phase), then do it with someone ideally outside the company ranks. You don't want to be later accused of causing dissent within the company or your team.

- Often when talking to friends, it's tempting to remain in the echo chamber, where you receive consolation and sympathy. But that's not the same as solving the problem. Find some trusted colleagues who can safely provide you with candid responses. I'm not saying this will be easy! You'll want to remain open, professional, and not defensive. You have invited them in, so don't chase them out!

- Once you feel more settled, it's time to go back to your manager with some questions. You want to avoid challenging them and things becoming hostile, so your questions should be targeted, clear and precise. For instance, 'You mentioned that my communications with my teammates didn't meet expectations, can you clarify where and how you think I could improve so I'm clear and then can focus on improving them?' And, 'Would you be able to provide feedback on a more regular basis?' Once a year I find is too long a span between feedback sessions.

❑ As part of your PDR, you may come out with some areas for improvement from your manager. Armed with the new information, be the bigger person and draw up a hit list of ways you can tackle the problem(s). When you're happy, email this to your manager asking them for their thoughts. This way, you have covered yourself and made your manager still feel in control.

❑ Change is hard. Be kind to yourself. You may change in a direction you didn't expect. Through your introspection and self-review, you may find that this job isn't what you want to be doing, you might see a glass ceiling above you or decide you want an organisation that fits more with your style. I'm not saying run away, but acknowledge that sometimes a square peg can't be squeezed into a round hole, no matter how you try.

 One thing I now do as a manager and you might suggest to yours, is to provide more regular informal check-ins. This way, issues to be solved feel small and achievable, rather than mountainous and overwhelming due to the build-up over time.

LEVEL
3.3

POWER UPS

SELF-CONFIDENCE

The biggest power up for an artist is achieving real self-confidence. A self-confident artist has a positive self-image, sets realistic expectations and goals, while communicating well and being able to deal with criticism. They can reflect on negative feedback without it crushing their artistic soul. But again, how possible is this to achieve? Many an artist has confidence issues and it's been a struggle for me at times during my career.

It's no secret that the mind can suffer from a constant stream of highs and lows because there's a nagging voice in your head, sapping your energy and dragging you down. I'm sure you've already had the conversation with yourself about how person X is better than you, their work is amazing and they always seem right. It makes you feel deflated or doubt your own abilities.

So, while it's a constant battle, you're not on your own, and there are plenty of supportive books on this subject. But I want to highlight three of the main downers here, ones I find crop up again and again. These common confidence killers can appear over the course of your development, so being aware of them from an early stage can give you the advantage.

Imposter syndrome – The voice in your head that picks on your errors and questions why you think you're good enough to be working in the games industry. It's the feeling that other people are more skilled and qualified when, really, you can do the job and just as well. Artists often find it happens at key points in their career, especially in a new role or line of work, where you must level up your skills, expand and grow into the unknown.

❏ In the past where team members have expressed these fears, they have already taken step one towards solving the problem. They have acknowledged it and, even more bravely, given it a voice. Fear of failure, or of being a fraud is best looked straight in the eye. What are you afraid of? Write it down, then write what you can do to get over that fear and who can support you.

Perfectionism – In our line of work, you can tinker away until you go mad. The first rule of artwork is that no piece is truly finished. Assets are completed either because of the deadline, or you've just had enough. I have perfectionist tendencies that I've learnt to modify for a greater sense of perspective; making games isn't saving lives, let's not kid ourselves, no matter what some of the fans might tell you. Artwork is subjective in the end but what or who defines 'good enough'?

❏ Your Art Director (AD) and Lead, with the help of the Principal, define the level of quality you'll need to achieve.

❏ Think of the project as a painting, only some of the assets will define the focus of the image. Likewise, most of the surrounding assets are there to support the hero pieces, therefore can be of lower quality. Not every asset can be a hero.

❏ It's natural to go chasing pixels, to craft and polish and obsess about whatever you work on, but ask yourself, is it worth it? Is your work recognised, do you feel like you're happy with it? Is your work/home life taking a hit? Are you happy with these costs? For most artists, achieving quality artwork is almost an obsession and it's easy to lose sight of what's important.

Know-it-alls (KIAs) – These people seem to have an opinion on everything, and a strong one at that, often leaving no room for others, never mind the chance of a healthy discussion. The impact can be large for a team, and can easily affect the whole team's morale, motivation, and creativity. Quieter, less dominant artists fear that the know-it-all will come along and tell them it should have been done a different way, and that other games did it better. Sound familiar?

❏ Often the KIA can have a good point, one that's worth listening to, but their terrible delivery lets them down. Try and look for the truth in what they're saying and ignore the condescending attitude.

- Sometimes the KIA can take advantage of an artist's low self-esteem, throwing ideas with passive, or just plain, aggression. Just because they are showering you with their knowledge and ideas, ask yourself, 'Does that make my ideas lesser?' Sometimes an answer is just different, not better. Avoid that thinking trap.

- The KIA likes to be asked their opinion. Go ahead, ask them what they think and sit back, you might get some ideas you can use and the other stuff, leave by the wayside.

- If your local KIA is becoming a major issue for your mental health or affecting your performance, check in with your manager to see what can be done to help improve the situation.

 Keep away from the people who want to bring you down, spend time with those who provide support and inspire you. You all rise together, celebrate the wins, move on from the mistakes.

CONFIDENCE BUILDING

With confidence killers out of the way, how do you build a more confident you? One who is more resilient to the outcome of making mistakes, and can put yourself in the spotlight or even promote your own achievements when it comes to review time? Think of confidence as a skill or even a muscle, with daily use and with healthy procedures in place, over time it'll become stronger and more resilient.

Recently, I had a big slump in my creative drive and confidence. While looking for a remedy on TEDx talks, I happened upon Dr Ivan Joseph https://www.youtube.com/watch?v=w-HYZv6HzAs. He was talking about confidence in athletes and how he coached them through difficult periods. It made a lot of sense, so I bought his book on Amazon; 'You Got This: Mastering the skill of self-confidence'. I can honestly say

> *that this book was crucial in turning my situation around, to looking at what I had, rather than what I didn't, to see the gaps in my life not as blank, but opportunities to fill. So, I did, writing, experimenting with 3D techniques, design ideas, making posters, planning and it all fed back into my professional life and rebuilt my confidence.*

So, what simple steps can you take to keep yourself moving forward, avoiding creative plateaus and more importantly, making the act of learning fun again?

1. Build your stage

2. Reflection

3. Identify your challenges

4. Plan your fun

5. Give yourself time to fail

6. Repeat

Build your stage – When I say build your stage, think of making yourself the star of the show. There's no audience, no pressure, but ask yourself what you need to make yourself comfortable and supported. Do you have all the equipment and software to be able to physically take on this job? Sometimes the smallest of things can stop you, like your mouse is a bit too small, your keyboard letter A doesn't work too well, or your chair is too low. Even minor irritations can trip you up.

What about your workspace or home office, does the environment make you feel comfortable? Can you make simple tweaks that will make you happy when you see them? Let's not forget the mental preparation too. The physical stuff is much easier for most. Imagine yourself as your best friend, how would you support them? You'd tell them nice things, you'd say, 'You can do this, just have a go, it doesn't matter if you make a mess'.

Thoughts influence your beliefs, which influence your actions (from Dr Joseph).

> *I'll let you into a secret, when I was writing this book and, in my recent slump, I realised I wanted to reduce the negative talk in my head. I printed out a page and stuck it on my wall, just behind my monitors, I see it every day, each morning when I come into my office and sit down for work – 'Paul, it's your time to shine'.*

Reflection – It's important you spend some time reflecting on yourself. Think about what you're good at, what you like, skills you want but don't feel you can achieve. Don't overthink it, be reactionary, and write down whatever comes into your head. The nagging voice in your head will try to persuade you not to do this. It's silly, why bother, that's easy, don't bother. Remember, it's your time to shine now, the nagging voice can carry on, but it sits in the corner away from you, you aren't listening any more!

Identify your challenges – You have your list of goodies to achieve; now it's time to break down what you need to get there. Do you need a particular book, a tutorial, do you know someone you can ask for help (and therefore show a vulnerability for some)? Have you got a good music playlist, do you need to go and buy some tasty ground coffee for the perfect cuppa?

Plan your fun – Pick one of your list of challenges. A small one and easy one. Don't go for the 'learn ZBrush'; if you listed that, it's not reasonable, it doesn't fit into the SMART system (see below) and only makes you feel overwhelmed.

Let's say you wrote, 'I want to learn how to make stylised artwork instead of realistic which I normally make'. So, imagine you want to build an old watermill with some set dressing (bicycle, bucket, old broken wooden cart). To make this easily achievable and fun, you'd start small and build up.

- ❑ **Specific – Make your goals specific and narrow to be effective.**
  (I want to make a real-time broken wooden cart, using substance painter.)

- **Measurable – Define how you'll prove you're making progress.**
  (White box, grey box, learn substance painter, final asset in engine.)

- **Attainable – Can you do this? Is it reasonable?**
  (I will do this in my spare time, two nights a week, but I can be flexible.)

- **Relevant – How relevant is this goal, how important is it?**
  (I want to improve my art skillset and improve my confidence in learning new things.)

- **Time-based – A realistic end date for you to work towards.**
  (In two months, I'd like to have this cart complete.)

Break your 'finding the fun' into mini milestones, so everything becomes easier and less overwhelming. When you complete each task, take a couple of minutes to reflect; how did it go, what did you learn? Are you further ahead in your knowledge and skill than you were an hour ago? Your progress might be slower than you want but it's not a race, this is about building you up, brick by brick.

> On Star Citizen, my producer and I at the start of the project had a phrase 'You can only eat an elephant one bite at a time'. You might want to sculpt an amazing character and it may seem an impossible amount of work, but any large complex thing is just made of many smaller tasks. Take them on, one by one. Don't rush and before you know it, you'll cross the finish line.

Give yourself time to fail – When I did this, art became fun again. If my work turns out crap or worse, only halfway good, I see now that it's ok, because I'm not running for artist of the year award and I don't claim to be the best. Finding ways to keep yourself motivated and curious is the greater part of this challenge. With curiosity you can remain fresh, push into new areas, try new art techniques and, if it all goes to shit, then it goes to shit and you start again (after examining where it went wrong).

Building up your own small areas of self-confidence will pay dividends.

- ❏ You'll start to recognise that with planning, time, and practice, you can do whatever you set your sights on.

- ❏ This will translate into work; you'll find your own inner artistic strength and that will project out to others.

- ❏ You might even find your work gets better. You'll have a greater positive mindset even in times of trouble and those dips we talked about at the start of this chapter will still appear, but their effect will be less severe and you'll recover faster.

Repeat – Your confidence will grow through repetition. No matter how many mistakes you feel you make, you are showing yourself you can push through to the end. Now, find another challenge, take it on to keep building yourself up and look to find the fun!

Reading this as a list seems straightforward doesn't it? Seems too simple in a way, yet many an artist will find excuses to avoid whatever it is they fear. But not you! Keep building yourself up, growing and becoming more resilient.

 You don't get to be excellent by focusing on the mistakes you made, it's by focusing on what you do well.

GENERALIST OR SPECIALIST?

As your career develops and you look to rank up, your skills grow, expand, and strengthen. Time spent at your desk will no doubt propel you in various directions; some you expect as you aim there deliberately, and some will be a surprise as the project creates new challenges. How you position yourself, how you utilise your new skills, will affect your career path. Eventually you'll come to a fork in the road. Let's look at your options.

Generalist – A good proportion of the art team is filled with generalists, and I would say that most artists start in this category, which is natural. You know a bit about everything, which means you have a strong foundation to build from. From here you can decide to continue to grow in all directions or focus in; there is no right or wrong here by the way.

Specialist – The other path you might choose would be to specialise. Say you pick character art, you might choose to specialise in sci-fi armour, or become the character head specialist, someone known to craft craniums, faces, hair, expressions, materials and so on, and make them the best in the business. Your other work might be good, but your specialism is where your talent and passion really shows.

In games, specialists are needed to provide the final layer of quality to your assets, so your specialist might be your Principal Artist or a seasoned Senior. They can help by informing the team about general improvements, or by taking what the other artists call 'done' and then giving them final polish, quality or delivery.

Combo(ist) – Ok, I made that up, but it works for this illustration! There's an area that I would define as a combination artist. Someone who didn't want to become a specialist because they enjoy the variety of working in different areas but can provide support and a high degree of art skills to anything they touch.

> *Because of the way I came to be a 3D Artist, by working on sports stadiums, flying logos, animated characters, promo pieces and many long nights of nursing rendering farms, I had gained a strong multi-disciplined skill-set, a mixture of art, animation and technical. As I mentioned at the beginning, I class myself as specialising in being a generalist, and I don't think I'd be an Art Director today if I didn't have this broad range of skills.*

> **TIP** There is no need to specialise right away, enjoy your journey first and foremost. Your specialism will develop over time and in areas that you naturally enjoy.

MENTORING

Would it be dramatic if I said this is the gateway drug to leadership and management? Mentoring is the soft option and I mean that in a good way. It provides the warm, fuzzy feel-good part of passing on some of your hard-earned knowledge, a way of working back and forth with people, no pressure, just good vibes from watching people grow and develop.

You might have guessed by now that I really like mentoring, it's my favourite part of the job. Even by the time you are a Mid-level Artist, you will have opportunities to mentor someone, and definitely when you become a Senior. But what does good mentoring look like, should you be doing it all the time and what if you suck at it?

What is mentoring?

Put simply, you're an experienced and trusted advisor. Your role as a mentor is to provide missing knowledge to help train less-experienced artists. Your tutoring can be unofficial (you do bits here and there) or official (your Lead asked you).

Who's involved?

You, the mentor, and the artist, the mentee.

What makes an ideal mentor?

I like to explain this using the three Cs. http://www.mentorsforum.co.uk/the-three-cs-of-mentoring.htm

- ❏ **Consultant** – Using your previous experience and knowledge, you can help reduce mistakes made by juniors or by those with less experience. Your insights can help the artist produce work faster and therefore make a better overall product for the company, not to mention a better experience for others involved in collaborating with that artist. Remember, often artists are working with designers, tech artists, VFX, coders, so reducing friction is always a good thing!

❏ **Counsellor** – Sometimes, you just have to sit back and listen. Your artist may be having issues other than their work, which they might not confide, or it could be just all work, work, work, and that's fine too. You want to give your mentee the space to explore and grow, point them in the right direction, show them the tools and let them crack on.

❏ **Cheerleader** – Praise is often overlooked, as we concentrate mainly on problems and finding solutions. But what about the good stuff, the well done, good job, looks sweet? Everyone needs some of this to balance out the process. Best not to be negative, even better, be comfortable giving constructive feedback as well as praise.

What makes an ideal mentee?

❏ Ask questions. You want to learn, right? So, ask questions! Game art is both so technical and so artistic, and there are many challenges and directions to take. If you're anything like my young self, you might get analysis paralysis. I would burn hours trying multiple different solutions instead of just asking someone. Asking doesn't make you weak, in fact you're being clever by saving time, because there are no prizes for slogging it out, not in this industry.

❏ Be receptive. If your mentor is giving advice, don't throw it away because you don't agree. It's good to talk through something that doesn't make sense or isn't clear. What have you got to lose? Try out the new method, give it a go, take it on if it works, or ditch it if not, but at least you tried and your mentor can see that.

❏ Communicate clearly if you request some mentor time, as chances are that you'll be pulling them away from something. Think ahead to determine what the precise question is, or the problem you are facing and how to articulate that. if your question is slightly vague, you might need someone to bounce it around with, to help fully define it. The main thing is you've done your homework, because turning up begging can only go so far. You ultimately want to be a solver, and it all gets noted when it comes to review time.

Common problems

My mentee won't listen – The artist you are trying to help always knows best; they want your help, yet can't seem to quite accept it. Sometimes an artist must learn the hard way. Ultimately, that's their issue and, again, it will be reflected in the performance review and assigned as a development opportunity.

I suck at mentoring – Ask yourself this: Do you? Do you really? Is your advice really that bad? Is the problem low self-esteem, even though your skills are highly developed? (The two can easily co-exist.) While mentoring might not come naturally to some, it's an enjoyable part of the role once you settle into it. Like all the skills needed to climb up the ladder, it's worth spending some time looking at the areas of yourself you can bolster instead of doing another hour surfing ArtStation.

Unrealistic expectations – These can come from either side, but I would expect mainly from the mentee. Every young artist wants to achieve more for less. They see others' amazing work after hours, days or weeks of practice and want to jump right to that stage. It doesn't happen, as I'm sure you already know, so the role of a good mentor in this case would be to help set expectations. Acknowledge the small wins and keep pushing the artist forward.

Poor matching – Often you don't get to choose either as a mentor or a mentee. It's usually the Lead who spots the problem and asks one of the team to help the struggling artist. There's a chance you won't click, and in this case, it's a matter of staying professional.

TIP No two artists are alike, so tailor your mentoring delivery to each person. Some artists require more cheerleading, while others hate it and will only want consultation to enable them to deliver results.

CRITIQUES

Part of being a good mentor and artist is the ability to give and take critiques. With artwork being so subjective, it's easy to get lost yourself and please excuse the cliché, but if you do that, you won't be able to see the forest for the trees!

Sometimes artists (and I've done it myself) can get so focused on solving a problem, making the geometry work, trying to hide a mistake, or massaging a UV coordinate, for example, that they completely miss that the asset is just plain wrong, so they're wasting time and effort. It's only when someone comes up and points out the major flaw that you can see it. It's so frustrating, but it can certainly happen.

You might get critiques from your friends, and you definitely will from your Lead/Art Director (AD). Everyone has an opinion on art and, while some are more valid than others, knowing how to give and take them is an important part of your career development. The skills that you develop in this arena go a long way to smoothing out your journey.

In an ideal world, you'd make artwork and it'd all be great, but so many combined elements contribute to how your work is deemed 'successful', including the subject, materials, proportions, technique. It's always best to seek a second opinion, which makes you a stronger and more versatile artist. I didn't take crits that well, because I was a perfectionist and used to hide my work away until it was nearly done, deliberately slaving away until it was too late. It would result in frustrating remakes and alterations. I've learned the hard way, but you don't have to.

Critique vs criticism, what's the difference? The two are so close in spelling, they could be the same thing, right? True, but they're not the same at all, in fact they couldn't be more opposite.

Criticism is something no one appreciates, it's potentially personal, destructive and damaging. It's a judgement whose focus is finding faults either with you, your work, or both. It is often based on the critic's self-importance, allowing them to feel better about themselves or cover their own inadequacies.

Critique is based on informed opinion, skill and is impersonal, it deals with the problem directly. Being constructive provides solutions to improve the artwork (not to just change it for change's sake). The feedback is most effective when it's targeted and avoids generalities.

Common mistakes

- Avoiding feedback. If you are anything like I was and avoid asking for advice until it is too late, then you might have a rude awakening. At all stages of your career, it's best to see feedback as a requisite for advancing. Why spend time making the same mistakes or hitting the same wall when you can ask for help?

- Being precious. Digital artwork enables you to craft, polish and tweak repeatedly. Being precious about your work gives the impression you are defensive and unwilling to budge. You might feel like your work is your best yet, but asking for input at an early stage could really make your work shine brighter.

Simple wins

- Get feedback in stages. The best way is to get input and critique in the early stages of development, and it's even better if you have multiple options to look over. Implementing feedback at the start of an asset is by far the cheapest option, because the further the asset gets developed, the more time will be needed to make expensive alterations. It can involve not just you and your team, but other departments, which is when things get expensive for the company.

- Feel the fear. You might want to rush ahead and do your thing because you feel you know best, but you may just be avoiding the fear factor. Once you see the value of, and can incorporate, feedback as part of your development process, it becomes something less scary and much more productive.

- Gratitude. You may or may not agree with the critique you receive, so it's ok to discuss it and have your opinion. But if your Lead or AD is asking for changes, then you'll want to implement them. If you get good advice, thank your reviewer. Everyone likes to be thanked and, in this industry, it's easy to overlook the small wins.

- Change can be hard, but it can be good. You might face new techniques that seem overwhelming. But broken down, they're a series of small tasks which link together. If you feel overwhelmed, make a list, and it doesn't matter if it seems stupid or feels like overkill; what's important is that you find a way to get over the hump and boosting your confidence in what you're doing. Practice cures all!

If you haven't gathered already, receiving and understanding critiques is one of the fastest ways to level up your artwork and improve your soft skills, like communication. If you've a trusted group to bounce your ideas and problems around with, then you are well on your way to progressing up this crazy career ladder.

LEVEL 3.4

POWER OUTS

TEMPTATIONS

Achieving a promotion is always a great feeling and reaching Senior or Principal Artist status is the culmination of thousands of hours of hard work, not just personally, but also professionally. You've invested in yourself, working to improve your art and technical skills. The reality is that good artists are hard to find and talented artists are always in demand. As the recruitment emails find their way to your inbox, the question inevitably arises, 'Am I happy where I am?'

Well, I'm glad you asked, and the answer to this career question is that you have four options; you can go **up**, **across**, **down** or **out**.

LinkedIn enquiries are probably landing in your email, containing tempting offers and tantalising deals from recruiters trying to land you for their next big deal. They might offer the proverbial golden carrot, promising a new and exciting land of opportunity. With the demand comes temptation. You start thinking, 'What if?', or 'Yes, more money would be good,' or 'I don't feel appreciated here,' or 'I want a more challenging project'. All valid thoughts, because as creatives, we want to feel challenged and to keep progressing. But ask yourself some searching questions before jumping the fence to that greener grass.

There's no judgement here on how you answer these questions, they are more for fact finding and soul searching. The more honest you are with yourself and the more authentic, the more likely you are to come to an answer that you weren't expecting and one that doesn't require you to move on.

- ❏ What are you looking for?

- ❏ What isn't your current company providing?

- ❏ Are you looking to escape something?

- ❏ Is your career path blocked?

- Are you creating your own blockage?

- Is it a financial, project or life decision?

- Are you running away from something or someone (bad boss or a bad situation)?

Let's step back and look at the four categories I mentioned previously:

Going up – Could you jump up a level? Even if you're at the top, you can still try to increase your salary or bonus level. Or you might want to go into the world of management and try your hand as a Lead Artist.

Going out – You might simply want a change, a fresh challenge, something that will help keep your skills sharp. It's possible to get pigeonholed, and sometimes it's easier to make a clean break to try that thing you've always wanted.

Going across – Not something to strive for necessarily, but it's often a natural part of development. Say you hit a plateau or decide to take a break from striving, coasting so to speak. This isn't a problem in the short term, and we've established we're not robots. Creating comes at a cost and you might want to replenish your artistic reserves for a time.

Going down – This might include hitting the wall. You like the company but are burnt out or don't agree with how the project is run but can't afford to move. This might lead you to turn to the dark side (losing your way/being unhelpful), which inevitably will affect your career/position/bonus unless you can turn it around.

From the company's point of view, it's important to retain good employees, and understandable given the years of training and knowledge of pipelines and complex techniques, which all can take a long time to impart to someone new. Ideally, if you're happy with your current company, speak with someone who matters to consider your options before deciding to take the leap elsewhere. It doesn't have to be a black and white world; it turns out it's mainly grey!

We've covered areas in which you overcome challenges to keep moving forward, progressing along your chosen career path. But sometimes situations happen, and you get stuck in a pit or your career shifts into reverse. While difficult, they aren't insurmountable. Let me tell you about burn-out.

BURN-OUT

Burn-out is a common problem within the creative industries, and I'm hoping that, with the advice in this book, you'll be able to take better care of yourself than I did and avoid it.

Looking back, my burn-out wasn't so much a quick intense flash but a long, slow fizzling out. It was a culmination of many factors, building up like water just before a major landslide. I was approaching 38, a date linked to my dad's age before he passed. I was starting to question the world, the corporate system and, while I undertook some counselling and career guidance, I was still very much a rebel without a clue.

With long hours, the demands I was putting on myself, my lack of management experience and missing mentorship, all took its toll. I felt I needed the equivalent of a shock and, seeing no way out that I'd be happy with, I gave myself the equivalent of artistic CPR. After leaving, it didn't get better initially, we packed up the house and moved back to England, ripping the kids from their school and friends of over six years. Honestly, I felt a shell of a person, guilt washing over me daily, the icing on the cake when we decided we couldn't bring the family dog back with us, the dog that the kids loved as a dear friend.

So, for me, I like to think I've had my moment. I call it a moment, but it spanned years and I thought at points that I'd never recover. Thankfully I did, after much reflection. I was never the same though, not in a bitter and twisted way thankfully, but in a way that I knew more about myself, about how to handle situations, about how to ask for help and, more importantly, to be a boss who has compassion and understanding, someone who can say 'I don't know,' but work with his team to find the answers. It's an ongoing process...

That's a bit depressing isn't it! Ok, let's look at how to turn this on its head. Let's look at identifying some common symptoms of burn-out. Burn-out refers to the smothering of a fire or the extinguishing of a candle. It implies that once a fire was burning, but cannot continue burning brightly unless there are sufficient resources that keep being replenished. https://www.wilmarschaufeli.nl/publications/Schaufeli/311.pdf I found this while researching, and I feel it totally nails it.

Your creativity grinds to a halt –This is the most obvious of the symptoms, and the most frustrating for an artist. You're sitting there just willing yourself to be creative, under the heavy expectation of the company and your previous achievements, but nothing comes out, and what does is lacklustre and uninspiring. You can feel others looking at you and thinking, man, this artist is just losing it, which of course compounds the problem.

Your gremlins start to take over –A war rages inside your head, good versus bad. Bad gaining ground daily, suddenly you feel like whatever you do is worthless, that others can do way better. The pressure mounts and starts to push any creativity further down into the void, meaning that risk-taking is a thing of the past, and your creative adventuring goes up in smoke. You know you really need to perform, otherwise your boss will review you negatively, but you just can't make it happen.

Your values alter – In this case, you're no longer aligned with the company and what they're trying to achieve. You become disengaged with the project and even staff, swag is no longer seen as a gift but as a bribe, and bonuses are golden handcuffs and not a genuine thank you. You feel like a cog in a machine.

Your health changes – Mental and physical problems can arise, comprising more trips to the doctor, lower immunity to disease, tiredness, anxiety, detachedness from family and friends, drinking more alcohol or drug-taking to numb the feelings of stress, weight gain or loss, irritable bowel, poor quality sleep, lack of self-care and appearance, and depression, among others. These are all examples of the issues commonly reported.

So, what next?

Though the revenue from gaming is huge, in contrast the gaming world is comparatively small, made up of a microcosm of game developers. For this reason, professionalism is key to a good exit. I made some clangers when I left companies, often just making up my mind and moving on, not even thanking my bosses. At the height of my burn-out, I walked out and never went back, surely the signs of a desperate man, and someone who just wanted to leave. But I don't recommend you do that, far from it, and there are much better ways of moving on.

When you have made the decision to move on, think about these things before handing in your notice.

Try to:

- ❏ Find a new job before handing in your notice. It's always easier when you are employed, and it provides a safety net if you don't get the job. It's also more attractive if you're still in a job to anyone searching, they won't have that question in the back of their mind 'What's wrong with them?'

- ❏ Avoid gossip about thinking of leaving. It's unprofessional because either you are, or you aren't, going to leave. If you are unhappy but don't want to leave, find someone to talk to, as there are often options that you haven't considered. Standing at the water cooler musing isn't solving anything, I'd call that fantasising.

- ❏ Gather everything you may need. You should assume that you'll have no, or restricted, access to anything once announcing your departure. Some companies are very strict and won't let you plug in USB devices, so there's a chance you can't take anything on leaving.
  - ❏ Do you have your own personal work on the company PC? Assuming it is permitted, move it over to your removable hard drive.
  - ❏ Clear your desktop/folders of anything that is personal to you.
  - ❏ Make note of contact details of the people you want to stay in touch with.

❑ Back your bookmarks up from your browser if you don't share across devices.

Definitely:

❑ Make an exit plan, figuring out when to go and how you would like to go.

❑ If you like your boss, tell them you're leaving in person rather than before sending the email. Give them the chance to talk it through with you because it's best to end on a high note.

❑ Prepare an exit email to send to the company, in which you should thank the good people, leave out the bad, and let them know where you can be contacted.

❑ Know the correct amount of notice according to your contract. If you have vacation days still owed, then the company can pay you for them or advance your leaving date by the number of days owed, so you leave earlier.

❑ Don't badmouth the company, boss or employees. You can do your reputation harm and find it more difficult to get another job.

❑ It's sad to leave friends behind, so celebrate and enjoy some quality time before the change. Often you find you'll be working with them again years later.

Then move on! Enjoy the challenge of the new job, city, or country, making new friends and working on new, fresh projects. Fan your creative spark, enjoy the new challenges, and find your next happy place.

LEVEL THREE SUMMARY

There's a trend happening here, do you see? There's a lot of information to acquire which forms the building blocks for life in the games industry! Time, effort, and dedication spent in this period of growth can define your future direction. It's not set in stone of course, you can make a change at any time if you are prepared to put the extra work in, and it's true that you get out what you put in!

In essence, this is the time to grab your career by the scruff of the neck, really taking charge of what sort of artist you want to become, pushing to get what you want and not expecting anyone to give you any free rides. This is down to you, so take advantage of what you now know and use the system to your advantage. If you've forgotten something on the way, no problem, let's recap before moving on.

3.1 Bigger, badder and better
- ❏ The three main production artist roles are Mid, Senior and Principal Artist.
- ❏ Did you find out what changes as you climb the art ladder? The interviews for each position will shine a light on real-life experiences.

3.2 Levelling up
- ❏ To level up, you need to get promoted and your yearly review is super important to that process.
- ❏ Know what areas of skill you'll be reviewed on, each of these require work.
- ❏ All set for the Personal Development Review? No? Well, go back and brush up!

3.3 Power ups

- ❑ Self-confidence and promotion are key to climbing the ladder more easily.
- ❑ Start to figure out where you excel and where to focus your efforts; will you choose to specialise or remain a generalist?
- ❑ Be the mentor you always wanted, help the whole team level up.
- ❑ Critique is not the same as being critical, so know the difference to keep your confidence high.

3.4 Power outs

- ❑ What do you want to do next? Have you thought about your career path and what keeps you happy?
- ❑ The threat of creative burn-out is a real issue, keep yourself safe.
- ❑ If you are thinking of moving to a new company, keep it professional, because you might need those connections later.

The three Mid to Senior roles form the backbone of the art team. Levelling up increases your exposure to more creative areas of the project with more responsibility and ownership. Also, your bank balance will be happy too. As your skills improve, so do the financial rewards with each promotion.

This period of growth is huge for any artist. You'll tuck some high-quality skills under your belt, pushing and developing into new areas and working on some major projects which will be released into the hands of the public. It's quite the rush when all the hard graft comes to fruition and you can showcase your artwork in the form of a released title. Time to celebrate!

After the dust has settled, title(s) under your belt, release parties over, you can allow yourself to wonder. Choose either to carry on as you are, making artwork, honing your skills and pushing your expertise, or start to consider new challenges, such as the Lead Artist position, which would be a step into a new world. Becoming a team leader, helping to shape the development of artists and artwork alike; it's a higher stakes position.

Are you ready to take that step?

WELCOME TO MANAGEMENT

Just like those crazy little dinosaurs from Bubble Bobble or the dynamic duo Mario and Yoshi, you're going to need every trick and power up to make the most of this next phase of your career journey; transitioning to Lead Artist and a management role.

Up to this point, you've been levelling up your art skills, taking on harder parts of the project, handling increasing pressure, giving estimates, and hitting deadlines. In the process, you've mentored Juniors or Mids and have taken responsibility for developing some critical areas of the art pipeline. But until now, it's all been about you.

When you become a Lead Artist, you'll undergo a transformation, one where your focus shifts from you and your skills to your team and their skills. Their wins become your wins and their losses become yours too. This change is one of the most radical and challenging for an artist, but also one of the most rewarding when it all comes together.

You are now transitioning into the domain of the mythological beast that is half artist, half manager. What would that be called? Artiger? Manatist?

Silly names aside, this is serious business and major changes are going to happen. Your brain will swell with so many new techniques you never knew you even needed! Ultimately, it's important to understand it will take time to practise these skills and adjust accordingly. Like your artwork, all this will require refinement, and sometimes you'll make mistakes. From those mistakes, you'll learn and improve your new craft.

As a Lead, there'll still be opportunities for you to get involved in artwork, but most of your time is devoted to other areas. In essence, your role is to focus on driving your team to make great assets (large or small) as smoothly as possible and help to develop the pipeline. You utilise your team as a master artisan would their workshop, a conductor their orchestra or a manager their football team.

Through this chapter, we'll delve deeper into what this role needs from you to succeed, but as you can see, there is no mention of artwork here. It's about really understanding yourself, your artists and how the Lead Artist role is pivotal to the team's success.

The skills we cover in this chapter are just the start. At the outset we're just scratching the surface, but by the time you reach the end of these topics, you'll know 100% more than I did when I started (I'm so envious of you right now!). Right away, you're already one step ahead of the game.

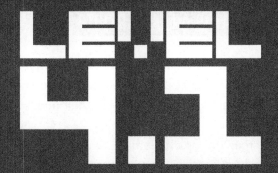

LEVEL 4.1

LEADERSHIP

WHAT IS A LEAD ARTIST?

I was a Lead Artist, so I'm going to impart what I know, what I've experienced and what I've seen. As you now know, all studios work slightly differently, tuning the role to their needs and those of the project.

I read this on the Gamasutra website, and think it's a great description. https://www.gamasutra.com/view/feature/131524/common_ methodologies_for_lead_.php

> 'The lead artist helps the team, technically and artistically, to carry out the art director's vision. The lead understands how to conserve where necessary and how to give more freedom to the areas that are important in achieving the goals of the game designer and the art director. The lead artist handles the technical aspects of the art team: art processes; tools; geometric budgets; texture budgets; task definitions; scheduling of tasks. The lead also communicates with the lead programmer and the producer to identify risk in the production pipeline. The lead takes the burden of artist management and protects the art team from counter-productivity'.

Now that sounds like a hefty role, but note that it's not all down to you. You aren't on your own, this role is about you and your team. You decide who does what, what's best for which artist and how to solve challenges collectively.

I found there was a strong temptation to be the superhero, that being the Lead Artist means you must be the best and know the most. While some people present that illusion to you, everyone has strengths and weaknesses. Being a good Lead Artist is knowing your boundaries and understanding how to work with your team; you'll work together to fill the gaps and put the pieces together.

Great expectations

I think it's important that you understand your role and how you fit with your team. I've broken it down into simpler, bite-size points.

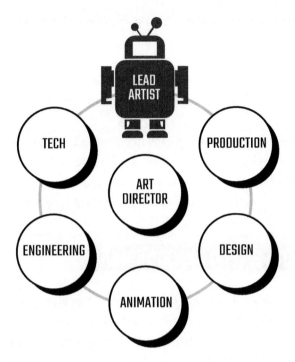

Figure 15. The art loop

- ❏ Support the AD in their decision making by offering advice and a sounding board.

- ❏ Work to create a well-oiled machine (be the grease, not the grit).

- ❏ Shield your team from any project turmoil.

- ❏ Between you and your team, work to create the AD's and the company's vision.

- ❏ Be ready to work harder than before.

- ❏ You can't be everyone's friend, but you can always be professional.

- ❏ It's ok not to know the answer to a problem, but find someone who does.

- Don't waste your time complaining about problems, find solutions and fix them.

- You are part of a loop, and if you can achieve synergy with the other departments, then you become a formidable team.

Ok, let's dig deeper into what it means to be a good Lead(er) Artist and the wider context. We'll think about which areas to develop, how to discover more about yourself as a young manager and what you can do to grow into this position, giving you and your team the best opportunity for success.

SLICE OF LIFE – LEAD ARTIST INSIGHT

Meet André, now working back in Sweden, he has worked on some major games, *Batman: Arkham City, Battlefield 4, Mirrors Edge Catalyst*. He's made the leap from full-time artist to Lead Artist and gives his insight to switching to this pivotal role.

Q. Let's start with the basics – who are you and how long have you been in the industry?

A. My name is André Wahlgren and I'm currently a lead level/environment artist. I've been in the industry for 13 years and counting now.

Q. You've worked at a variety of companies and countries, how was that experience and what did you think you would gain?

A. I didn't necessarily think about what I would gain when I applied for my first position abroad. I mostly wanted a job, but I do also remember that I was tired of Sweden and wanted to get away. I had been in a relationship that just ended and had no actual connection to any part of Sweden or town, as I had moved around a lot.

In retrospect, I think it was good for me to get out of my comfort zone and test new places. I also really enjoy some of the connections I've made through the years. For example, when I got married, I got a bottle of wine as a gift from an old friend I hadn't seen in 10 years.

I think going to a new country and working there is an incredible experience and something special for our industry. I really miss it and I think it's a shame I didn't do it a bit more. I learnt a lot, experienced a lot and even now I'd say most of my best friends are non-Swedes. I think it is confidence building.

Q. Did you notice any major differences between how studios operate?

A. I sure did. I've been at different places during different times in development. Some were more coordinated; some were a bit more rock 'n' roll and took it in their stride (generally these places had one person with the big vision that guided everyone).

At one place there was no strict task setup, so for some things you could come up with your own ideas and tasks and work on it until it was approved.

Q. The transition from senior artist to lead can be overwhelming, was that your experience – did you take baby steps or was it a sink-or-swim kind of situation?

A. I was hired as a lead to another studio, so I came in fresh to the team, the project, and the gig. It was definitely a sink-or-swim situation where I felt I had to live up to the ideals and image I had sold the people that interviewed me.

I had a very passionate view and opinion on how a lead should work and what they should do. I was being interviewed by two teams, one didn't want that version of a lead, and one that did.

It was definitely overwhelming; I would fall asleep before 8 in the evening for a long time. Just after the kids had fallen asleep.

Q. When you took the role, did you know what you were getting yourself into, were you fully aware of everything a lead had to deal with?

A. I had no idea. It's been very challenging, honestly. I don't know if it's because I set a high bar for myself and that I see a lot of things that I want to help out with or what.

Every studio runs the role differently, what I found the toughest at where I'm at now is the HR aspect. It's tough to keep a team motivated and happy at all times. Sometimes, you can't and that's very difficult to accept. So far, I've managed well, but it keeps you awake at night and distracted sometimes.

The "We need to talk" or "Do you have a minute?" always gets the blood pumping.

Q. How much help did you have in transitioning or were you self-sufficient? Was there anything that you look back on and think, 'oh if I'd only known that!'

A. I think I was very much on my own. I had my own sense of guidance and what I wanted to see in a lead. Sometimes during one-to-ones, I got asked for feedback but overall; I do think it's been a role of my making.

To me, I think the biggest lesson I've learnt is, being a lead doesn't mean that you have to be the best or know everything. You don't have to be the best at Z-brush; you don't need to be able to come up with an answer on the spot.

I think some people would argue with that but that's ok. That's my second lesson. You can't always be friends or in agreement with everyone. Game development is a compromise, in my opinion.

I definitely think having a lot of experience from different countries and studios has been super beneficial. Your team will come from all over the world, and I think it makes it easier for you to find middle ground.

Q. Has there been an area in this new role where you recognised you needed new and upgraded skills?

A. To loop back to a previous topic: The soft skills or the HR/Social aspect of the leadership role comes with a lot of things you've never really trained on in a studio environment.

- Speaking in front of people.

- Self confidence.

- Giving feedback in a constructive and positive way. How do you tell someone that they need to scrap a week's or a month's work in a good way?

- Social knowledge and empathy.

- Being calm and not getting pulled into a discussion or into a negative spiral when dealing with problematic team members or bad moods.

I think it's important to remember, but also sadly easy to forget, the being-human aspect.

Q. There can be a lot to think about as a lead, problems whirling about in your mind, what do you do to keep your head clear so you can sleep soundly at night, or do you wake up at 3 am like I did thinking about problems waiting for you that morning at work?

A. I got kids. Mostly, they keep me physically drained, so I pass out easily.

I think I'm the worst person to have gotten this question at this very moment.

It's a mix. Recently I've lately been working with a kind of career and life coach to become better at disconnecting from work mentally. It's a challenge. I've had that 3 am thing.

Sometimes I can play with my kids and have a blast, but then suddenly be thinking about what my team members should be doing or how to solve something. I've found that acknowledging it and brushing it to the side works the best.

"Yup, now I thought about work again, but it's not 9-5 so it's not your problem now."

Q. Would you describe your role as 50% art, 50% leadership? If not, what percentages would you assign to your current job?

A. I think 80% leadership and 20% art might be more aligned, there's not much hands-on work. It's about putting together material and guidance / feedback. My goal is to get up to 50/50.

Q. Have you done any reading around on the subject of leadership? If so, what books do you recommend to budding Lead Artists?

A. I don't have any links or books per se, but TED Talks and GDC talks have been super beneficial to me. I've also been meaning to read *Creativity INC* by Ed Catmull, which I hear is good.

Q. I think that the Lead Artist/Art Director relationship is one of the most pivotal to the project, would that be your view too?

A. Tough. The AD has the final say. I wouldn't feel comfortable going against feedback or direction. I would make suggestions or offer alternative solutions but if those don't work, it's still my job to help carry out the vision.

In general, I think it can happen quite often during a project, but bottom line is that it's all very subjective and a matter of taste/opinion. You should be professional enough to know that and move on.

Q. I read 'creation and maintenance of a prospering art culture' was part of your job description – how do you help maintain the culture or drive of the team?

A. I make sure to set up art meetings where we do show-and-tells, talk about new tools. Train each other, organize workshops. I also recommend material I've bought or seen that I think the studio would like. I also ensure we have access to good training material from different educational sources.

Sometimes we watch GDC talks with "Fika" (Cookies, coffee and treat; it's a Swedish thing).

I also think it's important that they see that I care about learning and try to keep my skills fresh too.

Q. Ok, let's not ignore the elephant in the room – let's talk 'crunch' – like it or loath it? Do you think it can be removed or reduced?

A. I don't like it, but I think it's necessary in small spurts. Having to crunch means we've failed somewhere, but having it in for a few weeks ahead of an E3 build or similar showcase is usually a nice bonding experience for the team and project. I also don't think you can get away fully from having it a bit at the end. There's always a bug to fix. I would advise against it. It does the body no good in long stretches.

Q. How do you balance your drive and keep motivated when times are tough?

A. I think I read somewhere that the "burnout" after 5 years and again after 10 years. I definitely have a bit of that going on right now. I'm looking internally these days at what I like to do and what I want to do. I've kept my head down for so long in the game dev sphere that it's tough to know what your identity or creative needs outside of it are.

I haven't found the answer, but I've noticed that I enjoy drawing and photography/cinematography. Telling stories and creating emotion. It quiets my overactive mind. I think finding those things dear to you that silence the noise in your head are the keys to maintaining your motivation and sanity.

I'm also dreaming a lot about the old days. When projects and teams were graspable. I don't think there's a big surprise in why many indie studios from old devs are popping up.

These days the projects are monumental efforts and beasts to tackle, and I don't know how feasible it is in the long run.

Q. When you look back and reflect on your career, any bits of advice or information you would have liked to have known back then when you were starting – what would young André thank you for?

A. I think the cliché statement of going out and experiencing your life is the biggest lesson. It will greatly influence your career and give you confidence. At the same time, Practice, Train, Study. Always.

I'm very happy about having been so focused on my art, on game creation and that I've been able to get as far as I have. Never stop learning. Allow yourself to get swept away. It doesn't always have to be about the things you do between 9-5 or have the same appearance or form. Learning can be different things, and everything will influence your work and being. I think that's key to staying on top of your game.

André Wahlgren
https://www.artstation.com/wahlgren

You'd be forgiven if you think I'd coached André for these answers as they line up so closely with all the topics in the Lead Artist chapter! I didn't! It's a challenge going from artist to manager, one that often requires some rearrangement of skills and approaches for you and the team you are working with. But fear not, I've some great information to keep you at the top of your game.

GOOD LEADERSHIP

Different people define leadership in different ways. My view is that there are inherent qualities to being a good leader. I look for the following qualities: someone who's dynamic, talented, interesting, caring, empathetic, who inspires the team to deliver and, finally, someone who can actively listen, and I can respect.

But how do these qualities play out in the role of Lead Artist? It's shielding your team from politics or poor decision making, giving your artists their time to shine, and assigning opportunities based on their strengths, even if they lack self-belief. Guiding large egos without crushing them, encouraging team creative skills, creating a consistently level playing field and showing no favouritism. You are the rock, a stable guiding influence, listening to the team, digesting that information, and implementing solutions. You don't forget the small things like giving thanks and celebrating achievements, such as hitting deadlines or delivering work, even though it's expected.

> *When some of my peers have progressed into a management role, they often say 'I had no idea that all this was going on, we were totally shielded from it all'. To me, that's affirmation of doing your job, a good job at that, in giving your team a calm space to hit their targets.*

Think of yourself as an umbrella, protecting your team from the challenges that rain down daily. There could be problems like illness, changes to the schedule, additional workload, torrents of emails, monthly, weekly, daily reports, conflict, quality issues, tech problems, ego wars, wage negotiations and so on.

Leadership isn't something that can be picked up as simply as a power up in a game; you can't suddenly choose to +1 yourself. It's more of a slow deliberate upgrade, a process of experience and reflected feedback, but don't worry, it doesn't have to be at glacial pace, there are tools out there to help you develop and speed up discovery.

This chapter is just a taster to discovering your leadership qualities; next we'll take it to the next level and focus on you. After that, we'll break down all the factors that influence a successful manager.

LEADERSHIP STYLE

It's hard to know what sort of leader you're going to be until the pressure starts to build. Tasking, art and tech pipeline, staffing, quality control, meetings and reviews will be the day-to-day challenges you'll face with your Art Director. You won't know how you'll perform until after the fact. However, you can do a little searching, to give yourself an advantage.

Often Lead Artists are elevated into this very different role but haven't asked themselves the pivotal question, 'What sort of leader do I want to be?' They tend to rush straight into the practical side, fighting fires and learning on the job, all the while ignoring one significant factor, how their personality will affect themselves, their team, and situations.

How you solve a challenge (people/art) depends on your thinking process, the outcome can significantly vary whether you class yourself as an introvert, extravert or ambivert. While these are umbrella terms (covering wide areas), they begin to help you figure out what sort of personality you have and how it'll interact with others.

Introvert or extravert?

One isn't better than the other, and there's no right or wrong, but it can affect who follows you naturally, and who might need extra effort, as we're all attracted to certain personality types, and yours will affect your management style.

Benefits of introverts

- ❏ Listening is higher on their agenda than talking.

- ❏ Spend time in their heads, keeping their thoughts to themselves until the time is right.

- ❏ Interactions with others require energy, so to recharge, they spend time with themselves.

- ❏ Often highly focused with an ability to concentrate for long periods of time.

- ❏ Considers the facts for longer before deciding on a course of action.

Benefits of extraverts

- ❏ Able to work the social situation easily, groups of people and gatherings are relatively easy.

- Gains energy from interactions with others.

- Often seen as good leaders by others (though leadership does not depend on being introvert or extravert).

- Can be seen to display greater levels of emotion and passion, this personality can draw others in.

- Makes decisions impulsively.

If you want to do some interesting research into yourself (I highly recommend it, it's eerily accurate and I tried it on my family too!), then try the first of these links. It's free (I'm not affiliated with either) to get an insight into your personality traits.

- 16 Personalities (https://www.16personalities.com – free service)

- Tilt 365 (https://www.tilt365.com – paid service)

> *I find 16 Personalities to be effective at clarifying what kind of person I am, how I work, and what my traits are. Tilt 365 helped when I was working with a career coach in the US; I had some hurdles with communication that I wanted help with, and it was a great introduction to understanding staff dynamics.*

What to do with the information

I hope that, by spending five minutes answering questions, and five more reading the answers, you've gained a greater understanding of yourself. To be an effective manager it's essential to know more about yourself than the people you work with (not just your art team, but the wider group).

By understanding how you operate and therefore what annoys you, it's easier to accept the ups and downs of game development. Problems no longer take you by surprise, giving you more control and time to create solutions.

TIP Be prepared, just because you've done your homework, it doesn't mean your boss will! They might be too busy, not interested or not bothered!

NOT ALL BOSSES ARE CREATED EQUAL

While you're pondering how to take the gaming world by storm with new ideas and ways to energise yourself and your team, one very real challenge needs to be recognised. Your boss and their bosses may be operating under the old ways and their management skills might be quite basic. Those in power have a comfortable job, often have no one pushing their soft skill development and, as a result, are less hungry to grow and develop these areas.

You have a good boss? Great!

A good boss is like gold in the bank. It can only be a good thing. Having a healthy working relationship with someone you respect and admire makes for a much more enjoyable role.

- ❏ As Lead Artist, your immediate boss is the Art Director (AD). But there will be people senior to your AD to be mindful of. They can influence your AD's life, which can affect yours.

- ❏ Watch and listen, to see their strengths and weaknesses. As you learn to predict their methods and thinking, it can make it easier on you and the artists.

- ❏ All ADs operate differently. This may sound obvious, but I've seen it catch people out, as they transfer from one studio culture to another.

- ❏ Some ADs are hands on, creating assets, especially if the team is small and tight knit. The larger the team, the more the AD will work with the concept team and look to you and the team to implement the vision.

- Work to complement your AD, because the best results happen when you collaborate as a dream team.

- Arrange weekly catch-ups with your AD to discuss the team, issues, and project. They might resist but you have to try!

You have a terrible boss? Boo!

Alas, there's a lot of poor-performing bosses out there, but that's why we have books like this, right? To raise the quality and improve the industry from within. Why some bosses are less than spectacular is a bit of a riddle, but in my travels a few things have stuck in my mind:

- Your boss might be old school, thinking 'Been there, done that, got the T-shirt' and be disinterested in improving their soft skills. They have reached the top, why push and refine those skills, after all, who can tell them to improve?

- They might be an awesome artist but bad at planning and people management.

- They could be a Technical Director who has been mis-hired.

- Boss not helpful? Look elsewhere, depending on what the issue is.

- Some bosses are bullies, who are sexist, racist, or homophobic. They create divisive and insecure working environments. A trip to HR could be the best route, but is not to be entered into lightly. If you find yourself in this position, ensure you gather evidence.

- If the issues feel insurmountable, something you can't control or influence, then you'll want to make an informed decision about moving on, to another team or company.

- Moving on is not a weakness, especially if you have exhausted all avenues. You aren't a robot, companies don't give out prizes for soldiering on, and eventually poor workplace life will affect your health. Don't wait for it, tackle it head on.

Ok, now we've got that elephant out of the way, let's continue with upgrading you.

LEADERSHIP AND MANAGEMENT TRAINING

These two should be like jelly and peanut butter, a perfect combo (if you like that), but are often more like oil and water. Companies might think, 'Well, our management don't seem broken, so why spend money on training?', not fully appreciating the benefit of levelling everyone's soft skills up.

Back in the day, team building was a trip to the pub. Then it progressed to paintball or building towers out of newspapers. You can understand why people weren't jumping and waving their hands in the air to get onto a training course back then, because it wasn't inspiring nor did it solve anything remotely useful for you, the new manager.

Thankfully, times are changing and new recruits expect more from their managers and for their own progression. The choice of courses is much greater for games companies now and much more easily tailored to the situation.

What are the benefits?
- Improved connection with the team.

- It's not just managing, it's coaching.

- Greater team engagement means happier artists.

- Staff retention. If your artists regularly leave, you've got trouble.

- Boosted self-confidence to handle difficult situations.

- ❏ Better evaluations and Personal Development Reviews of the team.

- ❏ Greater self-belief in how to move forward (fewer gremlins).

- ❏ Improved toolkit to spot team issues before they develop into something bigger.

- ❏ Communication skills upgrade.

What are your options?

Depending on the scale and revenue of your company, you'll have a range of options to choose from. The list below is arranged from cheapest to most expensive.

- ❏ Chat with your mentor, who may be your Art Director. Often, they will have experienced similar troubles and may be happy to share advice. If they aren't able, then try other more seasoned Leads; it's good to trade notes and techniques. Take care to keep confidential matters to yourself though, but you can still talk in generalities.

- ❏ Read. Make use of book services such as Kindle Unlimited; there are so many books with excellent advice to try out before you open your wallet wider. It's possible your company has resources available, so they may absorb the cost, the wider benefit being your team can also read the same books.

- ❏ Find out if the company would support some training. Before you do, try to identify what you are struggling with, because it's better to identify specific areas. That way you can get targeted support and make their lives easier when searching.

- ❏ Coaching. The company might provide this, or you may have to pay yourself. It's not a cheap service (I paid for it myself) but as you know, I found it super helpful, in getting over the hump and progressing again.

Take the initiative on this one and ask your boss for recommendations. If the company can't provide what you think you need, then it's time to be innovative. Find ways you can upgrade your own skills. It might be by taking courses, watching some TEDx talks, YouTube movies, LinkedIn training, whatever it takes; but treat it like any art skill you've worked on in the past. Help yourself become a leader and a good manager.

LEVEL
4.2

TEAM
DEVELOPMENT

GO TEAM!

We've covered you; we've covered your boss. Now it's time to meet the rest of your management role. This section looks at what happens when you join the team as a Lead Artist, new to the role of managing personalities, artwork and projects.

I expect you'll inherit an art team composed of mixed abilities and personalities. Part of your new role will be identifying artists on your team, those that are motivated and working well and the few who need help. So lets explore further whats involved in shaping your dream team:

- Personality wheel

- What makes a key employee?

- Creating inspiration

- Losing team members

- Conflict resolution

- Conducting Personal Development Reviews

- See a problem? Deal with it!

So, before you hide under a pile of schedules, meetings, pipelines and asset reviews, you'll want to get to know your team and understand how they operate. My biggest recommendation would be this: let your artists know more about you, then spend some time doing a little digging, finding nuggets of information about your team that will aid your leadership transition.

Arrange a meeting with the team and the Art Director, during which you can do a simple Q&A to let them know who you are, where you have come from, what you are looking forward to and how you operate. No messing, no guessing. It sounds stupid and overbearing, but done right, it helps set expectations for the team. Often frustrations can arise when artists think you should do or know something and can't understand why it's not happening to their liking (of course most won't voice this). By setting out your stall, there can be no misunderstandings. The added benefit is that this chat is the start of you defining your authority within the group.

 At desk, spend five or ten minutes with each artist getting to know their backgrounds, what they like doing and anything that they would like you to try to solve. Don't make the mistake of promising you'll fix everyone's problems, but if you see easy wins, get them in early to make a good impression.

 Send everyone an online questionnaire, and it's best if they are targeted. For example, pick which three things from a list they would like solved first (you might have been hired mid-way through a project).

I'm sure you can think of more or better. Not all companies will grant you the time (especially for Tip Two), and will want you to just 'get on with it'. But spending time at the start can reap rewards, when done well.

These are my recommendations for letting your team get to know you, setting expectations and making a good impression. Before doing your big sell, though, I suggest you read the whole of Level 4 for an overview of the challenges, starting with your art team.

PERSONALITY WHEEL

Understanding the make-up of your team is paramount. Skills are important too. But your team's personalities and how you combine and manage them are the key to a well-oiled art machine. Like a master baker, how you use and combine these top-tier ingredients can go well, or bring the whole team down.

In 4.1 we looked at Tilt 365 and 16 Personalities for evaluating your own personality and behaviours. These systems can be used for your team too, but in a more managed way. Being aware of the factors below can help you best decide how to solve your challenges. While no silver bullet, it's another part of your kit.

The industry standard for identifying personality types is the 'Myers Briggs Type Indicator', although opinion is divided on its usefulness. I see it as a possible part of your toolkit for understanding your team. The two American psychologists Myers and Briggs based their work on the findings of Carl Jung who believed that humans experience the world using four basic psychological functions: sensing, intuiting, feeling and thinking. Myers Briggs can be further researched here: https://www.myersbriggs. org/my-mbti-personality-type/mbti-basics/the-16-mbti-types.htm.

It describes the four pairs used for the test definitions shown in Figure 16:

❏ **Introversion/extraversion - (I/E)**

❏ **Sensation/intuition - (S/N)**

❏ **Thinking/feeling - (T/F)**

❏ **Judgement/perception - (J/P)**

EXTROVERTS (E)

Extroverts are energised by people, enjoy a variety of tasks, a quick pace, and are good at multitasking.

INTROVERTS (I)

Introverts often like working alone or in small groups, prefer a more deliberate pace, and like to focus on one task at a time.

SENSORS (S)

Sensors are realistic people who like to focus on the facts and details. They apply common sense and past experience to find practical solutions to problems.

INTUITIVES (N)

Intuitives prefer to fucus on possibilities and the big picture, easilly see patterns, value innovation, and seek creative solutions to problems.

THINKERS (T)

Thinkers tend to make their decisions using logical analysis, oobjectively weigh pros and cons, and value honesty, consistency and fairness.

FEELERS (F)

Feelers tend to be sensitive and cooperative, and decide based on their own personal values and how others will be affected by their actions.

JUDGERS (J)

Judgers tend to be organised and prepared, like to make and stick to plans, and are comfortable following most rules.

PERCEIVERS (P)

Perceivers prefer to keep their options open, like to be able to act spontaniously, and like to be flexible with making plans.

Figure 16. Personality types

This theory builds and expands upon our earlier venture into introverts and extraverts and their leadership styles. Using this builds more layers, nuance and understanding for you and your team. There is no good, bad, weak, or strong result. The Lead Artist role is all about making the best use of your team, fitting the right people together, reducing risk of conflict, improving team cohesion and bonding. At the end of the day, managing a team is no simple task and better armed is better prepared.

Clearly, I'm just brushing the surface of this subject and am no trained psychologist, but I see the value in observing the dynamics of the team and who works well with whom. It makes complete sense to choose my team with some additional knowledge of how they operate and if you can improve how you manage your team, why wouldn't you?

Now that you understand a little more about behaviours, let's look at how your team might operate and identify the heavy hitters, sliders, and workers you've inherited.

THE ART HIVE

Imagine the team you work with is a hive, in which everyone has a role to play. As the Lead Artist you'll notice how your team works, their ability, their commitment, and how they react to changes of direction, stress and organisational skills.

You'll quickly flag a who's who in your mind. This is important as you want to play your team to their strengths, knowing which artists can deliver based on minimal guidance, who can deal with complex tasks, who is more technical, and who is more artistic. You also need to know who does the bare minimum, who might struggle, and who are the heavy hitters and supporters. These notes will help you define the organisation of your team.

I couldn't resist using these definitions as often a hard-working artist can be known as a 'good worker bee'. Also, I'm in Manchester, where the city emblem is the bee! However, standard practice or not, it's a simple method of classifying your artists (in your head).

Worker Bee – These are the artists who day-in and day-out deliver the goods; you can give them any task and it gets done. It might not be award-winning art, but it's good enough for the game and sits well with other assets. They play nice with others and know how to work with a pipeline and other team members.

Killer Bee – Also known as a heavy hitter. These are the artists who you know, given any task, can make amazing artwork both visually and technically. You give them minimal information and boom, something magical appears. Any task, no matter what, short deadline, impossible task, they just kill it, time after time.

Queen Bee – The Art Director (AD).

Right-Hand Bee – That would be you, the Lead Artist, working with the AD and pushing the team to achieve what's needed for the project.

Sickly Bee – The artist who isn't pulling their weight. They ultimately let the others carry the load by working slowly, delivering subpar artwork, missing deadlines, or infecting the group with a negative attitude. Team morale is an important part of how well your team operates and how much work they deliver. If you don't deal with it, it won't go unnoticed and can affect your standing within the group.

 If your team isn't working, identify the reason and switch it up. With the AD, you're part of the long-term vision, don't be afraid of being flexible. The definition of insanity is doing the same thing over and over and expecting different results, so make changes where you need, mixing it up to get new results!

On the topic of morale, a motivated team can achieve far more than a downbeat one for obvious reasons. You are part of that mix. With help from the AD, you can work to create strong team cohesion and turn them into an art-making machine!

TEAM COHESION

Go team? High fives? Chuggin' beer? Standing in the park capturing Pokémon? What does it take to achieve the active ingredients that make some teams go far and fast? Well, it's not as simple as that, as what I've described is more team morale than cohesion. While morale plays a good part in this, there are some stages to consider when teams are formed with the common goal of making a game.

Let's start with the fundamental question: what does team cohesion mean? It's best described as when a team works together to solve a common goal, each feeling they've been able to contribute, which builds high levels of satisfaction, self-esteem and confidence. Ask Bruce, he knows all about it!

While 1965 seems like another world away, Bruce Tuckman must have hit upon something fundamental; a good part of the world appears still to be working to his theory that group dynamics have five stages of development, all of which play a part in the success of your team. Like other aspects I've mentioned in this book, I see this as guiding theory, something to be aware of as the project progresses. It is a process and not necessarily something you can achieve immediately. Instead, organically and naturally try to foster it so the team does the growing themselves.

Figure 17. Team development

In my experience, Figure 17 doesn't always happen as clearly and linearly. Teams can ebb and flow, sometimes regressing, and sometimes it's hard to identify the specific issue. Normally there's something fundamental going on (overwork, sickly bee, poor management) if you look closely.

1. Forming

This one isn't rocket science. When you bring a new team together, it might be an all-new team for a start-up or a mix and match of old and new artists. All these talents and personalities take time to settle in. It's a stage of discovery during which both you, the Lead Artist, and Art Director will be under assessment in the team's collective mind. They'll be looking to you for leadership, as the project is in its infancy and full of uncertainties.

2. Storming

In the storming stage, the team has moved past the awkward forming stage, they're familiar with each other and who are the strongest and weakest members of the team. Like a family, the team becomes emboldened, comfortable showing more of their true nature, opposing views, pushing boundaries. Clear leadership needs to provide direction, listening to all views, but not bowing to the loudest or most troublesome.

This sounds like a classic pre-production stage to me. I've experienced both sides of this coin, and when not managed properly, the team tears itself apart and collapses. When managed with clear and direct leadership/decision making, the team comes out stronger and more united.

3. Norming

Moving from competing against each other, the team works as one unit. Leadership roles are accepted, artists understand where they can pull and push and what's acceptable. Processes are becoming stabler and more established, including pipelines and lines of communication. Artists bond and mutual respect builds, enabling a safer environment for asking for help, for passing on knowledge to lift the entire team rather than the individual.

4. Performing

Full steam ahead, all systems are go. Your art team is absolutely nailing it, pushing boundaries of art, building assets, hitting deadlines; they can see, touch and feel the game's vision. Artists are happy taking on further responsibility and are more agile, able to jump between tasks. Your role is clear, the team understands what you do day to day, and what is needed in terms of quality and pace.

This is a great stage to be in. The team sustains its own momentum from their successes, because seeing all the artwork being built and implemented is fuel for the mind. When Epic formed Scion Studios for *Unreal Championship* 2, I remember this stage clearly. We were on fire, which is probably how we got a ground-up game built in two years with a team of 20 staff.

5. Adjourning

The game ships, and there's no artwork to be built until the next project starts up. It's a time of reflection. If there was a hard push at the end (bad crunch), there will undoubtedly be some losses because of burn-out. Ideally the team will transition onto another project together, maintaining the momentum and collective knowledge from the past game.

This is like the life cycle of an artist, isn't it? The benefit of this approach is it helps to understand and evaluate team development. The team is constantly evolving, both the people and the project alike.

For me, the one thing that stands out is clear and consistent leadership. Assuming you and your Art Director share similar values, you can provide the foundation for the team to grow in the right direction. The artwork is normally the easy side of the project, it's the team dynamics that have to be cultivated. By dealing with issues early on, having constructive debate, where opposing ideas lead to new ideas and coloration, you'll be well on your way to a healthy team.

But your team doesn't need to be continuously monitored. Once they're working well, they're self-running to a large degree. That's not to say you should be hands off and let it go wild, even the best-oiled machine needs some tweaking. For artists, inspiration and motivation are their fuel, so what can you do to keep them topped up?

INSPIRATION AND MOTIVATION

Inspiring teams can be hard, especially if they are a grizzled bunch of veterans, but regardless of your team's experience, you can still inspire them! But what can you do to get the team going and power them on?

A motivated team will move mountains. They might groan a little, but once moving, the impossible becomes the possible. I've seen it time and time again, where the project makes a big shift and the teams have to accommodate it and you know what, it all works out, everyone is motivated to keep the project rolling and to make a better product.

Before we look at motivation, let's clarify something fundamental.

What is inspiration? Inspiration is being mentally stimulated to do or feel something, often something creative. It's the spark that goes off in your head, you know, that moment where you think, 'Oh, I'm going to have a go at that!'

Motivation is not inspiration. Inspiration is the 'aha' moment, while motivation is the will to complete a task. You can be motivated to solve a tricky issue, but you'll need a moment of inspiration to provide the creative solution everyone is looking for.

Team motivation

- ❏ **Concept artwork** – For any artist, seeing some amazing concept art for the project really gets the blood pumping. Concept art sells a vision of the game that everyone can buy into, assets that they can imagine building, getting kudos and satisfaction from translating the ideas into a fully realised version. Often, artists will fight (not literally) to build the latest and coolest design.

- ❏ **New software** – There's nothing like a new tool, plugin, or programme to get artists inspired to try new techniques. Once one person has success, it's like wildfire and everyone wants a go.

- **New hardware** – There's a new ultra-wide screen, sure let's try it; new digital tablet, yeah, I'll give that a go; better noise-cancelling headphones, count me in! Who doesn't want the latest goodies and, for artists, a rig that improves speed and workflow is always appreciated.

- **Tutorials** – The only problem is choice, but that's not really a problem, is it? If your company has the budget, see what you can get assigned to you and your team, because more knowledge can only benefit the project in the long run.

- **TV/cinema/streaming/on-line shows** – A lot of studios allow streaming of shows while working (though normally in a small window). It helps pass the time on the long and boring parts of the pipeline and can aid focus for others. Movies and 'making of' segments are always a favourite too.

- **Other artists** –Examining other artists' work, whether digital or traditional media, all feeds into the mental bonus pot, the one you draw upon when creating your own creations and designs. For a team, it's good to have knowledge-sharing sessions, where artists share techniques on design theory, artwork, and software.

- **Interests** – Can your company provide life drawing classes or painting? It's always good to move away from the digital space, to make the brain work in other ways to aid flexibility of thought.

- **Trips out** – Reference gathering, go-karting, architecture, the beach, the bar, or whatever works for your type of team and project, you might even want to visit a museum or art gallery!

Fail freely

Your team needs to know it's ok to fail, which can be hard in a pressured environment, but if you can, give them some time to experiment and innovate. You never know what they'll come up with. Some of it could be junk, or so crazy that it inspires further discussion, thought, and more experimentation.

DELEGATION

If you aren't delegating, you're doing your job wrong.

One of the biggest myths of being a Lead Artist is that you must be the best artist. Absolutely, you need to be good at your job and, at the time of moving into the role, you might have the best skills in one area over the rest of the team. There's no question that this helps with team cohesion and respect. But because most people don't know what's involved in being a Lead, they have misconceptions about the role.

I mentioned previously that your focus must change from you to them, because you are there to manage the team, to maximise their strengths and remedy their weaknesses. Your role is master juggler, working out how to keep the project flowing while switching from one thing to another.

Not delegating is an easy trap to fall into, and often relates to control. You think you'd have less influence, or no ownership. At a fundamental ego level, you can't say 'This bit is mine', so you hang onto things, or your perfectionism gets in the way and, in the worst case, you become the pinch point. Imagine a wide river full of game assets floating down to a lock (that's you) but the gate only opens when each piece has been checked. However, the river at the gate is narrow and shallow, and checking is slow. You can imagine the chaos that reigns. Assets would back up, projects slow, bosses get unhappy, and the next thing you know, you're called into the office for 'the chat'.

For those to yet experience team leadership, let's look at few things to help you along the way, break down a few myths and give you something to hang your thoughts on.

Isn't delegation the same as dumping?

Dumping is the definition of poor management. It really should be avoided. As an employee, being dumped on feels like it sounds and only creates negative feelings and bad will.

- ❏ Unreasonable deadlines

- ❏ Little to no detail of requirements

- ❏ Minimal to no support

- ❏ No reviews until the end

So, what is delegation?

You are passing on work to others, but it's how it's done that's different. It's using the right person for the job and providing support.

- ❏ Manageable deadline

- ❏ Clear expectations of delivery and scope of work

- ❏ Supportive throughout the task

- ❏ Regular review gates

Is there a delegation process?

Yes, I think Figure 18 describes it well. Find the right artist with the right ability, brief them so they know what to do, ask if anything might block them and off they go! Then follow up with a review and provide feedback. In the workplace this is normal, and often work is reviewed as a group (art team meeting) or at the desk for one-on-one feedback.

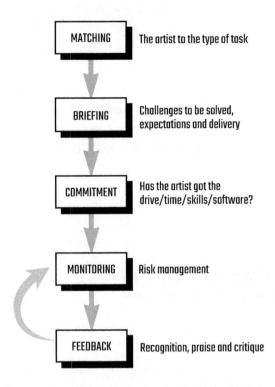

Figure 18: The delegation process (adapted from source: https://www.pocketbook.co.uk/blog/tag/delegate/)

I can feel you nodding off here. If you're wondering what the point of all this is, it's this: If you take nothing else away with you in this section, consider these points:

Delegation·

- Frees up time for you to concentrate on other important things

- Maximises artist engagement and pro-activity

- Boosts creativity and efficiency

- Shares accountability for the project where everyone handles something

- Shows cooperation and team building

TIP There's an old saying 'If you want anything done, ask a busy person to do it'. Delegate your work to team members who are already in the flow of pumping out artwork, already getting things done. They are capable and approach challenges with a positive attitude. There's one caveat though, don't overload your busy artists, otherwise, they'll burn out. It's a delicate balance!

This brings me neatly to the feedback process, how to offer critique and keep your team on track.

THE FEEDBACK PROCESS

One size does not fit all, and feedback is best when you tailor it for your artists. It's all too easy, especially if you have a large team, to approach them all in the same fashion. But have you noticed, some you get on famously with, while some hate you with a passion? Why is your management style working for some and not others?

Every member of your team is different, they all have different backgrounds, home lives, personal issues, health problems, confidence levels, experience and values. At any point any of these can change which will affect their work/behaviour.

Going back to the Tilt 365 system or Myers Briggs, can you recognise where your team members might fit? Understanding what motivates your team will help you get favourable responses from them. Depending on your artists' own journeys, they'll be at different points, so different levels of response and style are needed.

What stage is your artist at?

- ❑ **Approval** – Early-career artists are often looking for approval and support. Feedback can feel personal and they can react defensively. Some may have trouble sharing work and ideas for fear of making mistakes or receiving critique.

- **Apprentice** – Having overcome defensiveness and vulnerability, they are open to feedback, and are keen to improve their industry skills wherever they can. Eager to share and continue to build confidence.

- **Autonomy** – The artist has hit their stride; they are confident in their choices, regardless of whether others think they are right or wrong. Changes are accepted as part of the approval process, and they no longer take feedback personally.

Depending on your artists' own personal and creative journeys, you'll find that each one has a different story to tell. To get the best from your team, understanding them and how they operate certainly will help. But it's not a one-way street, and most of the time it's fairly obvious what stage an artist is at after your first few interactions. You'll see right away how they respond to your feedback.

Some of your team will be Juniors and respond well to gentle coaching, while others will be more attracted to direct talk about technical tasks. In which case, they'll prefer more specific instructions without vagueness.

> I had a habit of saying 'Maybe you could do this, or maybe try this'. While I felt I was clear about what I was asking for, some artists saw it as an option and it'd create confusion for them. It would create disappointment for me as I thought I'd given simple, clear direction when in fact I hadn't. I didn't want to give a direct command; what if it was wrong, what if it turned out bad, what if I'd wasted their time, how foolish would I feel? I'm sure you are familiar with these kinds of thoughts. Over time, my confidence has grown, and this is no longer an issue.

Common pitfalls of the beginner manager

I know quite a few of these because I've made them and fell into these pits. I can only apologise profusely to any of my past teams for having to endure this. But, like I say, you don't know what you don't know, sometimes you can't help making mistakes.

Next we'll look at some common sticky situations. These can increase your workload and restrict your ability to give clear feedback, reducing the effectiveness of what you're trying to convey to your artists.

- **Shit sandwich** – A classic early manager mistake. This is an overly used and abused technique. You start and end your conversation with something positive, but in the middle you sandwich the negative points. There's a hope your artist won't feel bad but that's all they'll remember after you walk away. The technique is used often because there's a vacuum of good alternative information or training.
  - Starting with the good makes sense, to appreciate and vocalise what you like and what's been done well. Then move onto areas for improvement and why, focusing on what they can do to achieve the 'correct' asset. Provide support, not derision. You don't need to end with a false feelgood quip, as that undoes any previous good work.

- **Getting your own way** – A new manager can fall into the trap of wanting to get their own way at any cost, because by not doing so, they think they're a weak leader. The downside is that other team members' feelings and ideas are pushed to the side, causing a lack of engagement as individuals realise they're not being listened to.
  - The strength of a leader is to recognise the best method, solution or idea, even when it's not their own, and take that one forward. It's much better to make use of multiple brains than just one. Even though artist X has the better idea, it's still your choice to make use of it. Once you start feeling powered up by your wins in decision making, you'll gain confidence in your leadership skills and you won't feel you're lacking control.

- **Perfectionism** – Our jobs as artists encourage perfectionism. We can undo any single action we make, make revisions, tweaks, improvements and alterations, but artwork remains subjective so there is no perfect. Chasing your vision of perfect is really costly, in time, energy and company money.

- ❏ I'm all for making great-looking art but you have to realise that the end user, the player, won't notice the final 10% (some may disagree here). It's a balance but deadlines have a way of reducing perfectionism.

- ❏ **Holding on too tight** – You want to keep control of everything as much as possible, afraid that if you reduce control, quality will slip. This causes you to become a bottleneck and assign yourself too much work, causing overload and team resentment.
  - ❏ Keep artists in your 'cone of vision'. I've used this method and passed it onto others. Your cone of vision defines the boundaries of what you are prepared to accept in terms of quality, style, technical set-up or whatever's important to you (it's important that you are clear before you can operate this technique).
  - ❏ This worked well for me as a way of loosening control over a team, reducing the urge to check everything, to constantly feel you should be on top of everything. With a big team, that's not possible.
  - ❏ It's about putting the responsibility on the artist. If they move too far away from the target artwork then they'll have to rework it to bring it closer. It doesn't have to be spot on, not everyone can hit the bull's eye, but as long as it's close and doesn't move the artwork too far away from the general direction the game is going, then great, move on!
  - ❏ I realise this makes no sense without a diagram...

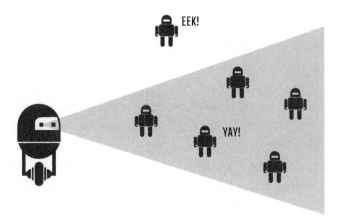

Figure 19. The cone of vision

- **Avoiding problems** – Even experienced managers can feel intimidated by the more difficult problems, things that involve unfamiliar soft skills, tackling under-performing artists, or team morale issues, and so they avoid doing anything hoping that somehow it will go away or resolve itself.
  - If it helps at all, these problems never resolve themselves. Left alone, they just get worse. They are only solved by you helping them along. Work with your Art Director (AD) and HR if need be, tackle them head on (but don't butt heads) to redirect and resolve the best you can. Sometimes you'll have employees who like to test boundaries so it's down to you and the AD to gently reinforce them.

- **Taking on other people's problems** – Another classic trap is where someone is all too happy to highlight an issue and then pass it on to someone else. As a manager, it's easy to try to be the hero and take on the issue so you can deliver thoughtful feedback, but what happens when there are too many to handle?
  - To answer this classic problem, there is a classic book in The one-minute manager meets the monkey by Ken Blanchard. Basically, the monkey represents a problem, and when you take on someone else's problem, you carry the monkey on your back. Too many monkeys, too much stress, and too much doing other people's work.
  - Once you recognise the people who pass on monkeys (can be anyone within the company hierarchy), then you can redirect or not even take the monkey on. This is one skill to learn if you're overly a 'yes' person. Be discerning about where you spend your time because it's precious.

Giving feedback is an art in itself; if it comes naturally to you and people accept it, then great job, you're a step ahead already. For some, though, it'll take more effort to craft this skill. Over time, you'll need to decide what works not just for your team but also for you to feel confident and secure. You'll make thousands of decisions over the course of the project and some will go better than others, but with every step of the way, you'll be improving. That's all part of the game dev process.

UNSTICKING THE STUCK

Having a mixed team of skills, abilities, and experience levels, you'll find the tempo will fluctuate over the course of the project. There'll be periods where everything is super smooth, and assets and levels all come together to make the magic. And there'll be times where some things start to wobble, wheels (artists) squeak, fall off or come to a halt, and as a leader, it's up to you to figure out how to free them up and help them run smoothly again.

You'll make judgement calls on the relative severity of a problem, considering how often it recurs, how it affects the team, and whether you even need to solve it yourself. Maybe a Senior should educate the others in the team, or even flag it and raise it with HR? You'll be making these observations and adjusting all the time. I've found team members fall into three categories, which'll help you in figuring out the right course of action and severity.

A traffic-light system works well, whereby you make calls based on the seriousness of the situation. While the problem severity will vary, one thing is certain, whatever the level, you need to deal with it!

- **Green** – Small tweaks, easy alteration, keep going (normal feedback)
  - I call these course corrections. It's the everyday stuff of being a Lead, evaluating work and making subtle corrections to hit the required quality bar for the company. You make hundreds in a week and keep the project progressing. The artists pick up on their mistakes and 99% of them avoid making them again.

- **Amber** – Needs observation, mistakes recur, or performance is declining (may need an intervention)
  - This level is normally saved for the repeat offender, and it may stem from a behaviour problem, but is more likely a procedure and art issue that the artist just isn't getting.
  - To solve this, I work with the person myself or assign someone to do daily or thrice weekly check-ins at a consistent time. This takes place for about two to four weeks and enables the artist to

realign, figure out what's going wrong and understand what's expected to deliver acceptable work. They can be five-minute chats at the desk, reviewing work, answering any issues, pointing out anything that could be a problem down the line.

❏ You're helping them, not just leaving them be and hoping they'll fix it, that's the difference here.

❏ **Red** – Inappropriate or unprofessional behaviour, stop and implement solution (private one-on-one, HR, or both)

❏ If your artist in special measures can't make the change, then it's onto a performance plan as a last resort (see below). Of course, if your artist has showed highly unprofessional behaviour, then it's time to speak to your artist in a private space like a side office to find out the facts and decide how to move forward. They must know that this won't be tolerated and continuing almost certainly will affect their current job.

When you've noted who needs help and the level of severity, there are a few things to think about to keep yourself on steady ground. Sure, you're their Lead, but you want to be well prepared, and for it not just to become a power struggle.

❏ **Identify** – Where does the person need help? This could include productivity, attitude, politics, time keeping, file management, or communication.

❏ **Check yourself** – Before you call the meeting, are you mentally in the right place? Are you bubbling over with frustration? If so, today is not the day to talk to your misplaced team member.

❏ **Keep to the facts** – Steer clear of generalities because it weakens your position when discussing the issue at hand. Avoid saying things like 'You always do this', which are vague and hard for the person to understand. Be specific, such as 'When you did this, that happened, and the consequence of that was this'. I'm sure you get the drift. You can't argue with the facts.

- **Keep it informal** – Until you don't, that is. Depending where on the traffic-light system an issue falls, it'll dictate how you handle the situation. If it's a first-time problem, then go in gentle and easy, perhaps in an off-the-cuff meeting, like a quick five-minute chat in a meeting room to consider the issue you'd like fixed. Should the task be more serious, or the person is a repeat offender, schedule thirty minutes and arrange it in advance to give your team member time to prepare (mentally).

- **Paper trail** – Always follow up with an email after a chat about something serious. You'll both have a record then. Also, they can suggest corrections should something not be reported correctly. I would also inform your HR Department.

- **Performance plan** – I saved this for last because it's the last chance saloon. When one of your art team consistently isn't hitting expectations (you may inherit them from a previous manager, so don't beat yourself up) then it's time to make a formal plan of action. It's painful and slow. All their work is measured and logged, everything is tracked and reviewed. From a Lead Artist's point of view, it's a proper time sink. From your artist's point of view, performance plans can go one of two ways; they improve and succeed, or they continue to stay down, and it's only a quick step to being released from their job.

THE PDR MEETING – MANAGER EDITION

In earlier chapters, we covered the Personal Development Review (PDR), which is commonly used as a yearly review of an artist's progress and development. This time we are looking at it from your perspective, as Lead Artist and manager. I've yet to see any training on how to hold a review meeting of a member of your team, it's all been learned on the job which seems weird, right?

Pre-preparation – This isn't for the actual review; this is your ongoing note-taking as you go along. With so much information flowing about, it's easy to forget the good and the not so good of your team. I recommend making a cheat sheet as you work through the year, divided into two columns, one noting areas of improvement and, just as importantly, areas where an artist really did well. Believe me, it'll save you a lot of time with filling in review sheets.

Review systems – I have mixed feelings about review systems. Companies use different systems, different rating schemes, numbers, words, you name it; it seems to be out there. Some review schemes are top down, in which your boss reviews you, you review your team. There is also the 360-degree review whereby your boss reviews you, you review the team, the team reviews you, you review your boss.

Get feedback – Either way, you'll want to get feedback on your team from others, whether they be other artists, designers, or producers, to obtain a rounded picture of how your team operates. With this information, you can complete your review of your team.

Follow up – If the review goes well for your artist, everyone walks away happy. Your artist may come out under a dark cloud, however. Follow up with the help they need; solutions will have been part of your discussion, be that mentoring, tutorials, or adjustments to attitude, but hold them accountable and keep checking in or assign a Senior Artist to help and provide feedback to you.

Quick tips

- ❏ Unsure of how to review? Ask for help, training, or have your Art Director there with you.

- ❏ Don't leave reviews until the last minute, it's not fair on either of you.

- ❏ Go in looking for positives, but don't shy away from areas of improvement and development.

- Ask questions, let your artist do the talking, helping them along with open-ended questions if they are the quiet type.

- Be supportive, as all issues can be solved, but their monkey isn't yours to hold, let them keep hold of it.

- Give them the opportunity to give feedback on you, ask them are they getting what they need, anything you can do more of or better? It's a tough one initially to ask, but like your art, you'll go from strength to strength as time passes.

LOSING TEAM MEMBERS

Whether you have helped shape a team or inherited one, it hurts to lose artists from your group. It's natural for people to come and go, and change is inevitable, because artists are hungry for more, for different projects, a higher salary, or an improved lifestyle. I did the same. But it's still difficult when someone asks you, 'Have you got five minutes?' You know something is coming!

In an ideal world, you'd keep your team, it'd be one big happy family (sometimes it is) but in this competitive world, things aren't that simple. Artists more than ever can join and leave for a variety of reasons, and they do, especially when unhappy. Let's look over some of the common reasons for churn.

- **Variety** – Artists are always looking to grow, wanting new skills and exciting opportunities. Over time, projects can lose their shine and artists want to challenge themselves in new ways, they might want to change from say, prop artist to concept artist. Sometimes, it makes more sense to change company to create the chance.

- **Boredom** – Artists like to get titles under their belts, to work on engaging projects, and to show their work. If the project is floundering or career progression is limited, artists can get itchy feet and start to look elsewhere. If there's another more successful project being made down the road or in the same town, you can bet your bottom dollar they'll look to shift to the other side.

- ❑ **Poor management** – Your team may leave because of poor leadership; nothing loses staff at a greater rate than mismanagement of the team and project. As a middle manager, your reach within the company might be limited, but that doesn't mean you can't help in your own way. By identifying any areas that you can directly influence, it's possible to help improve the overall system.

- ❑ **Competition** – Are your staff leaving to go to other companies? See if you can find out why. What's making them decide to leave, is it the benefits? Salary? Company culture? The lure of prestige projects?

- ❑ **Lower pay** – This is easy to understand, more so in the UK. If one of your team is leaving and you really want them to stay, speak to your Art Director (AD), as companies can counter-offer and raise a salary to compete, hoping to make your artist change their mind. It's not guaranteed though.

- ❑ **Look closer to home** – Is it you? Can you do anything more, or better? Find out from HR or your AD if there are areas you could tweak in case you are causing friction.

Your team demands your attention just as much as any artwork, so keeping them motivated is important to the project's success. You can only do what is in your sphere of influence though, some issues are bigger and could be company culture–relate. The aim isn't to burn yourself out trying to be 'super Lead', but to have a growing awareness of your team and how they best operate.

You might have at least once thought, 'Where will I find the time?' It's challenging, especially if you're committed to a healthy work-life balance. So, my last chapter for Lead Artists includes ways to help you regain that precious resource, time.

LEVEL 4.3

TIME AND PROCESS MANAGEMENT

THE BIG (TIME) SUCK

By far the rarest of all your commodities will be time. There aren't enough hours in the day and that's why you'll need all your management skills to carve out time to do the important things.

What with context switching (changing tasks), interruptions from the team, bosses, messaging apps, email, real life, family, art meetings and team management, it's easy to be overwhelmed and feel slowly worn down, like being nibbled to death by a thousand ducks.

Fear not! There is light at the end of the tunnel. There are simple processes you can put in place to help yourself out, improving the quality of the entire team in the long run. Read these two lines and you'll be on your way to looking after yourself and your time.

Remember this: There will always be too much work.

And then this: Prioritise time for yourself.

I can't stress how important understanding this is. Give yourself time to breathe, to plan and to execute. The next few pages outline some methods I used to get back on top regardless of what the day had in store for me. I could work out a task list, attend my meetings, and get some artwork done. I developed these techniques as an AD, but they'll work just as easily for you as Lead Artist.

- ❏ Create boundaries
- ❏ Prioritise yourself
- ❏ Track your time and effort
- ❏ Learn how to plan effectively

I predominantly worked in large open-plan offices, which are great for team communication and for a manager to see what their team is working on. The downside is that you're accessible to everyone, all the time, increasing the chances of being interrupted on someone's whim (especially if they ignore the headphones-on rule).

So, let's find out how I used the techniques above and how they might work for you.

BOUNDARIES

On starting work, are you instantly swamped from the minute you log on? Do you struggle to think for yourself and get clarity away from distractions? Do you beg to be left alone, and all this before you get your first coffee/tea?

I'm normally later to start work than most of my team (and I leave later). It takes me a bit of time to wind up, but your team might already be working and in full flow by the time you switch on your PC. Great that they're eager and working already, but bad because there's a slow and steady backlog of issues for you to look over already.

An early lesson in management is to set boundaries. It's for you, your team, and the company.

- ❏ **Make some rules** – Think of it like this, you're a critical component to the smooth working of this art machine, and to do your best, you need to treat yourself like you would one of your staff (with compassion). So, allow yourself the time to settle in before the day whisks you away in a flurry of problems.

- ❏ **Settling-in period** – Mine was simple, it was this (and still is): No tea? No questions! Until I have a cup of tea in my hand and my computer is on, then no questions can be asked of me and there can be no interruptions. Please don't bug me about problems or issues or anything until I've had the chance to settle in and get my head in the game.

- ❏ **Time slots** – Rather than your team interrupting your train of thought at any point, you have the option of assigning some slots in the day, in which it's your time to concentrate, with no interruptions. This will allow you to plan and get ahead or do some artwork.

❑ **Communicate** – Always let your team know the rules by which you are operating. Give them fair warning if you are going to change the system. While you and the AD have to be super agile, your team may feel less flexible.

That's what I did, and it sounds simple, right? It is simple, and it was super effective. I'm sure you'll find ways that work for you, and these things don't have to be set in stone. If something isn't working, change it up! That's the wonder of being a team leader, you can make changes and be agile. Your job is to keep the art mojo flowing, and that includes you!

Some people feel uncomfortable making simple rules like this, but it's all about boundaries. You set them, you expect people to follow them. If someone comes to you before you are ready, unless their expression says that they are about to die as they have deleted the whole of the project, then it can wait and you can politely say, 'I'm getting my tea, settling in and I'll be with you shortly'.

(NB. You can't pull this trick with your own boss unfortunately – that's a one-way street!)

PRIORITISE YOURSELF

It's normal for a team to have a shared calendar to allow producers to know what you're doing in your day. If large group meetings are being arranged, the calendar shows when everyone is free.

This is both a blessing and a curse. The upside is booking meetings fast with no need to ask when everyone is free, but the downside is that meetings can fill up your day. Left unchecked, you can experience days where you don't have any time to do anything creative or for high-level thinking.

I book appointments into my calendar, because that way I can control my day and week to a certain extent, enabling me to assign blocks of time to get tasks done. This gives me permission not to rush through a task, as before this I often experienced a large unseen pressure to get things done as quickly as possible, because of the volume of other tasks waiting.

My other strategy was to book a 30-minute slot in a meeting room, just for me and for my morning planning session.

Me time (with my cup of tea) – I figured out that if I took my laptop and tea to a small meeting room for only 30 minutes, I could plan out my day. This is what I would do at the height of the chaos:

- Scan emails to quickly review for anything 'on fire', that needs attention.

- Scan meetings booked for that day/week, making note of any requiring preparation.

- Work out a prioritised task list for the day. I recommend choosing three tasks, and if you can get them done, then you are doing well (if your calendar is busy).

- Note down who you need to speak to that day.

- Schedule appointments in your own calendar to assign the three tasks for that day.

Doing this gives you full knowledge of your priorities so you can push back on any tasks should someone try to add extra to your day, particularly anything of a lower priority. Of course, this isn't foolproof, and there may be meetings that are just higher priority, which you'll have to make way for.

Overall, I find these simple techniques the best method for staying sane and on track, plus keeping overall anxiety at bay, so I could regain focus and start ticking items off my task list.

TRACKING YOUR TIME

It's good to know where you're spending your time. On the one hand, you might be working hard and just want to track the hours logged, but on the other, you might find yourself constantly flitting from one task to another and losing time from context switching.

You might want some extra data to help optimise your working process, to figure out where you are losing time due to interruptions, how to better estimate task deadlines and when your most creative time of day occurs.

Outlook – A recent addition to your email client now helps with monitoring and managing time tasks and meetings. Outlook sends emails informing you of your recent activity, who you spent time with, where your most productive time was, where most interruptions were, and whether tasks have been completed. It's simple but effective.

Company tracker – Your organisation might operate some sort of check in/check out software, logging when you start your day, when you have lunch, when you leave, maybe even when you have a comfort break. It can feel a little big brother initially, but you soon get used to it.

ManicTime – More for freelancers, but a useful tool in your management kitbag. It sits in the background tracking your workday, files, software used, proportion of your day spent in meetings. Non-intrusive and easy to use, with added benefits of graphs for data analysis. The free-to-use version provides the basics, which can be enough, but the paid version offers additional insights into your working life. (I'm not endorsed by ManicTime!)

You'll want to check with your IT department before installing software, to make sure your data is protected, and that they're happy to have the software on one of their machines.

Give it a go to see where you are spending your time. You might be pleasantly surprised and find some extra ways of making your days more productive with fewer interruptions. Or realise that a task takes double the time to complete than you normally estimate.

TASK PLANNING

As a Lead Artist, you'll spend plenty of time planning your team's workload. You want your team to be effective, happy and productive, so how do you get ahead of the curve?

Simple! Plan, then plan some more!

One of my favourite quotes is 'failure to plan is planning to fail' (credited to Benjamin Franklin). It's true; how can you hope to succeed if your plan is non-existent? Some companies attempt to wing it and then spend their time in crunch. Games are complex, which no one is denying, but there are ways of planning and estimating that can improve your art team's work life. The goal is to provide a steady stream of work with a few peaks but little wasted effort overall. If only it were simple and straightforward...

❑ **There's no perfect plan** – This goes without saying. You won't know all the details of the project, and there will be some guesstimating based on previous experience. However, everything can and should be broken down into a series of tasks. Working with your Producer and Art Director you can figure out an initial master plan.

❑ **Time-boxing** – A simple method for estimating the time needed for each stage of the process, taken from the Agile Scrum framework. On past projects, I have time-boxed levels and assets and it proved to be highly effective. For example, it would look something like this:

- Block-out art – 2 weeks
- First pass art – 4 weeks
- Hero asset creation – 4 weeks
- Second pass art – 4 weeks
- Polish – 2 weeks

If necessary, it can be more granular and apply to an individual asset, say a space crate or suit of armour, but how granular is often down to how the company runs.

- **Plan B** – Always have a back-up plan, because you can bet your house that your original plan will change, whether it is by an executive, publisher, or a re-prioritisation of team members.

- **Buffer** – When you are estimating time, it's natural to underestimate, not to consider possible problems (you can't know the future, but could you have foreseen some of them?) or to fail to account for the interruptions and time lost for context switching. So, one standard practice is to build in a small buffer of (extra) time, especially for large complex assets. Your artists might not know you have a buffer, and sometimes it's hidden. An artist's instinct is always to fill up the time assigned, making their artwork as strong as possible.

- **Prepare to be agile** – You want your senior artists to be flexible, so let them know that. You don't want team members who constantly create blockages or are inflexible. There are always options and solutions, which not everyone might like, but with your producer's help, it's up to you and your team to come up with the magic plan of action, with built-in options!

There are so many books out there to help you with your task planning, so I've kept this section simple, short and to the point. Planning, like artwork, is something to be practised and polished, and, while at first it might feel foreign, you'll soon become expert at the Excel sheet.

LEVEL FOUR SUMMARY

So, are you now ready to take the bull by the horns? Becoming a Lead Artist is like entering a brave new world, where even armed with all this information, you are going to be required to make changes of yourself, to have buttons pushed you never knew existed. Rest assured, though, that this is your pathway to learning about becoming a coach and a leader.

Of course, I can't do it all for you, you'll have to find your own rhythms by working with your team and management. If you think about it, how many lead art roles do you see in the world compared with the number of jobs there are out there? Very few! This is a special role for sure and done well is hugely rewarding.

Let's round up what we've just covered.

4.1 Leadership

- ❏ Understanding what a Lead Artist is – half leader, half artist.
- ❏ Do you consider yourself to be an introvert or extravert, or a bit of both?
- ❏ Finding your leadership style takes time, so be prepared to change.
- ❏ Bosses aren't always good leaders, so it's important to recognise the good from the bad.
- ❏ Training to be a better boss is the right thing to do.

4.2 Team development

- ❏ Settle into your team, define where to push, where to pull.
- ❏ Learn to identify your team members' personality types. It'll help with team cohesion and problem solving.
- ❏ What kind of bees do you have on your team, are they all buzzing?
- ❏ Is your team all pulling in the same direction?
- ❏ Providing inspiration and motivation are key factors for a productive art department.
- ❏ Delegate, to clear time for yourself, to plan and produce art.
- ❏ Giving feedback usefully is critical, and a soft skill that's just as valuable as artwork.

- Be prepared to put the time in to support your team, to create a smooth operation.
- Giving artist reviews can be scary, but with practice and preparation – you got this!
- If you're losing artists, is there anything you can do to stop the leak?

4.3 Time and process management

- Setting boundaries is a key survival skill.
- Create a quiet space for yourself, some way of carving out time to think and plan effectively without distraction.
- Tracking your own time has its upsides, you can determine where all that effort is going.
- Plan, plan, plan. Can I make it any clearer? Then make a plan B!

The Lead Artist role isn't for everybody, as it clearly requires a different set of skills than you may previously have used. But if you like the challenge, the buzz of running a team and having a larger stake in the project's development, this is the job for you.

While your art skills might develop more slowly from here on out, your soft skills, like leadership and coaching, will grow apace. Factor in some good mentorship from your Art Director, and the project can only get better and stronger as you work together. No one ever said it would be easy. I just hope I've been able to supply some much-needed information to get you ahead.

I must mention, too, that it's possible you try your hand at this role and decide it's not for you. You can go up and you can go down or sideways, and up again if you want. I went back to being a Senior Artist for a while and enjoyed it thoroughly, as it gave me a chance to recharge and strengthen my art skills again, making more time for me and building confidence.

It wasn't long though before I started my push for the Art Director role I longed to try. Call it luck, call it fate, call it what you like, but it wasn't long before the opportunity came knocking. If you have your eye on that prize, you'll want to know the rules of the competition you'll be entering. Make no mistake, it's tough, so let's find out what's in store as Art Director.

LEVEL

05

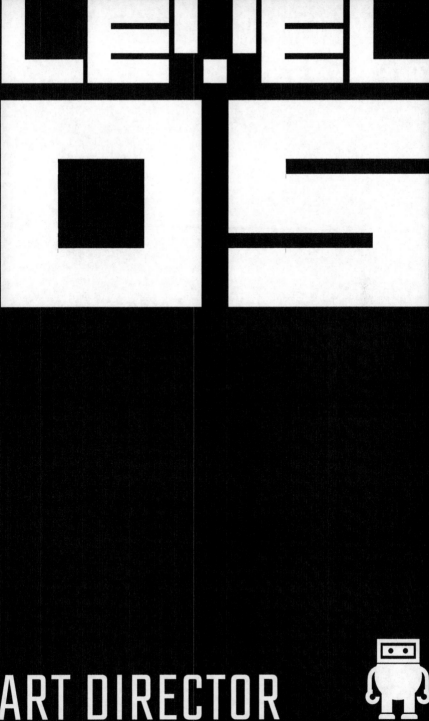

ART DIRECTOR

WELCOME TO THE BIG TIME

Congratulations! You've made it all the way to Art Director (AD). Now you can boss people around, doodle all day and hide away in your office surfing the internet! Joke! This is where the hard graft really starts.

Now you're fully into the big leagues and the pressure is on! It's time to take everything you've picked up on your adventure and really apply it, because your company is relying on you to craft the next great game.

The step from Senior Artist to Lead is a big one, no, make that a huge one. Now you'll find that the step from Lead Artist to Art Director is equal in size but has a different nature. If you're new to the industry, I imagine this section feels a long way away, but I wanted to cover this so you understand what an Art Director does for the team and what could be in store for you. At the very least, you'll have an insight into the inner workings.

Artists reach this role at different rates, and as I expressed earlier in this book, it's not a race. Some people are just naturally further ahead. There are situations where certain artists are elevated early because the company is rapidly expanding, and positions need to be filled quickly. At other times, a company might want to hire from within to keep an artist motivated. Much depends on the company culture and finances.

I wanted to be an Art Director for a long time. After working with talented Concept Artists at Epic Games, I really got hooked. When I realised I could directly shape worlds through other people's fingers, I realised that, even though my art skills weren't to the same level; I knew what I wanted to achieve, and they would take it and make it even better.

Getting my chance on LEGO Undercover City, while on the opposite end of the artistic spectrum, was a real challenge, mainly in scope but also because it was the first time I could put all lessons I'd learned to use in one place, to work on shaping a team, keeping motivated, improving my communication skills and ultimately producing a quality title.

I'll be honest and have said this before, you don't know what you don't know. When I took the offer of Art Director for Squadron 42 at Cloud Imperium Games, I was gung-ho and a little glib. I thought, sure, I can do this, sci-fi? Love it! Build a brand-new team – oh yeah, bring it on! In any normal situation, it would have been challenging. But a new team spread over four countries, making two products, on a new engine, on a massive scale with regular sales events, that's the perfect storm and not for the fainthearted! It's no wonder there are now seven Art Directors at the time of writing this.

Previous chapters have been retrospective, taking all my lessons and experience and distilling them into the straight up, no-nonsense content you have read so far. As for this chapter? Well, I'm still doing it, still learning even after over ten years, so I'm going to keep this high level to give you an idea of what could be involved based on what I've seen and done. Will it differ from others' experiences at other companies? Oh yes! The common denominators are grit, hard work and a talented team, the rest is just good luck.

I can honestly say I've learnt as much in this period as in my entire career before it. That might appear dramatic but it's true, and when you read on, you'll find out why. Here are some areas we'll cover to whet your appetite.

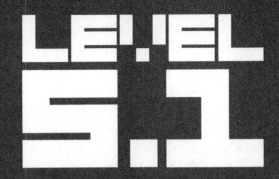

LEVEL 5.1

OVERVIEW

These four sections will give you a strong understanding of the director role for the story in this book, this is the final push, the last section of the journey to the top of the artistic mountain. But life doesn't end when you get to the top, in fact, you could ask, does anyone get to the top? Does the top even exist? Who decides where the top is? All philosophical questions, but ultimately everyone has their own idea of where their journey completes.

For some directors, they remain happy where they are, staying at a company for well over a decade. Others have itchy feet and move about enjoying the challenge of new projects and IPs. Art Directors often switch from working for a large multi-national to building a start-up company, hoping to recreate simpler and less corporate times. Everyone's journey is different, it's more of a matter of choice – where do you want your life to take you?

If you're not quite at that point as a new AD, you still have to prove yourself. It's not a time to slap yourself on the back (though it is well deserved) and kick back, this phase of your career is about to take off. It's a time for large amounts of collaboration with even bigger players and to push your skill sets to even greater heights.

Now you'll build on all the skills you've amassed. If you've skipped the chapters about being a Lead or experiencing a leadership role, I highly recommend you make your way back to the Lead Artist section, it's packed full of topics you're going to want to level up, to make the best of your Art Director opportunity.

WHAT IS AN ART DIRECTOR (AD)?

The lure of the Art Director role sure is attractive, and like a general commanding your armies, you can help create and destroy worlds, imagine new and unseen places, and craft visions of heroes and enemies, not quite at the sweep of a pen but close enough!

You'll be working closely with top-tier people in the company to create something new and exciting for the world's gamers, all the while working hand in hand with the Creative Director. This is an unavoidable tussle of collaboration and negotiation; pushing to get what you want and pulling back where it doesn't fit the game's overall vision.

> 'The art director is the creative visionary, responsible for defining the visual direction of the project. What colors will define the mood of the environment? What level of detail should the textures convey? What are the buildings in a city supposed to look like? How does the terrain look on this level? What kind of ambient characters populate this world? How red should the blood be? The art director works closely with the game designer to shape the game world. The art director carries the burden of communicating his or her vision of the game design to a diverse team of artists'. https://www.gamasutra.com/view/feature/131524/common_methodologies_for_lead_.php

If you look at any AD job description, it contains a formidable list of requirements. The company would like you to do almost anything and everything, and it might feel a little daunting when you first step into the role, but with a strong core team to support you, and the power of delegation, between you and your team, the magic will happen.

My aim is to give you a more authentic behind-the-scenes peek into the AD role, revealing that no two directors are alike and that ultimately, you'll need a blend of many skills. If you were a superhero, you'd have many heads and many arms and many super powers!

- ❏ **A visionary** –You'll be required to define the vision using your own skill, and with the help of your outstanding concept team. Along with your art skills, you'll spend a good portion of your week in meetings, managing the daily fires and issues that crop up during a project, reviewing artwork and pipeline decisions and maintaining balance within the team.

- **A leader** – Leading from the front, and ever the professional, you'll help set the standard for the team to meet or rise above. You'll need to build upon all the hard work you've put into developing your soft skills. If you make a mistake, own it, accept it, move on. If you get a win, celebrate it, however small.

- **A top communicator** – You'll communicate your ideas up to your bosses and down to your team, listening to both the good and the bad, dealing with the irate, and the less than professional when they have their moments. You'll be developing visual guides to define the artistic parameters of this brave new world you're crafting.

- **A collaborator** – You'll work cross discipline and with multiple directors, all with their own agendas, motivations, style of communication (or lack of) and politics. It is possible to be authentic and kind while still maintaining your authority. Note that you can't move forward without their support; the team must move together as one to make the best product.

- **A motivator** – Your team will look to you to set standards for art, behaviour and quality, as well as providing encouragement. Artists want to know they are doing well and where they can develop. On the flip side, when team members fail, you are there to provide support and help them improve.

- **A quality controller** – The buck stops with you. If areas of the artwork look to be of inferior quality, then your challenge is to identify them, find the origin and find a solution, working with your art team.

- **An educator** – You handle your team's artistic and mental wellbeing. You'll have access to a budget for buying books, movies, tutorials and software. If team members need coaching, mentoring or management training, you have the power to implement that. It's not all work, work, work, and you are also responsible for helping with team morale, meals out, trips to the bar and reference gathering trips.

- **A scheduler** – Your Leads will have done the heavy lifting of making a best guess schedule, so it's down to you to cast an experienced eye over it, identifying bloat and areas that can be trimmed, making sure important areas have room to breathe and grow. You'll want to avoid cutting corners where it really matters.

- **A tight-rope walker** – With all the above, it's a challenging walk you make every day, pushing your team, helping them to grow, and presenting your ideas and vision. All the while, you'll have to consider other people's wishes to make the game the best it can be, while maintaining your sanity and the ability to tackle the hurdles which will come your way. It's your job to find solutions.

- **A hirer and firer** – You'll be building, maintaining and trimming teams.

- **Not a Creative Director** – Often mistaken by others. But the Creative Director is above you in the corporate ranks. They are looking wider and further afield than just artwork. They're concerned with all the departments working together to create the right gameplay experience for the gamer.

This role is the culmination of everything you've learned so far and we're about to cover who you'll be working with on the project and how that affects you day to day. But before we do, enjoy reading this next slice of life as you really get an understanding of the variety within the AD role.

SLICE OF LIFE – ART DIRECTOR INSIGHT

Sadly, this is the last of the interviews in the book, but I hope you've found them as interesting as I have, providing a wider picture of the varied landscape called game development. Happily, this is a great one to end on.

I worked with Jerry at Scion and Epic Games, he's the ultimate go-getter in my mind, someone really driven to push the boundaries of what we understand as the world of game art. Jerry is an extremely experienced

AD and thrives on breaking new ground. Don't just take my word for it, it's clear in his answers – read on!

Q. Who are you and how long have you been in the Art Director role?

A. I'm Jeremiah O'Flaherty and I've been making games for over thirty years now. From platformers, to RTSs, to FP Shooters, to MMOs, to megahits like Gears of War, I've had the good fortune to get to work on a large variety of projects across a host of aesthetic styles.

A film school kid who fell into making video games at the dawn of home computers, I've ridden the wave of technologies that have constantly redefined what good looks like and what the future could mean for entertainment and video games. Winning an Emmy for the Augmented Reality Dragon at the League of Legends World Finals in 2017 felt like a fun exclamation point on a career always striving to push the technology just a little further than had been done before. Pushing to the forefront can also come with failure, which I have done many times, but I wouldn't give up the rush of giving players and viewers alike something unexpected and beyond what they thought possible with technology in that moment.

I've been a concept artist, an animator, a modeller, a VFX artist, a lighter, a camera specialist, but for the last 20+ years I've mostly been an Art Director. First at a small studio that a friend and I started, then to higher and higher profile companies running multiple teams across entire studios.

Art Directors come in all shapes and sizes and everyone's path is different. I've worked with amazing ADs who are Concept Artists, some are Modellers, others Graphic Designers, still more are Animators, and while all of them approach the role with different perspectives, it's always with the same goal of elevating a creative idea to its maximum potential through art and motion.

I happen to be a generalist who started out in the industry when one or two artists would make the art for an entire game. I had to learn all the tools and crafts to accomplish the desired goal. Luckily, I loved, and still love, learning new technologies and art apps.

Q. **What would you say were your super-powers in this role? You've extensive experience. What would others say you do well?**

A. Experience is definitely a massive part of the tool bag I use daily. The tools, technologies, and styles I've been able to work with and on make for a great perspective on whatever we are working at the moment. I never siloed for too long at any company, on any project or any technology.

I've come to figure out that I have to have a career shift/reset every two to three years or I go nuts. At Epic that reset happened when we shipped Unreal Championship 2 and the team was joined with the larger Epic team to make Gears of War. I was able to spend five years at Epic because I got to work on three amazing projects with the, at the time, brand new tech of Unreal Engine 3(UE3). This mix of emergent technology, the challenge of shipping a console-defining visual experience, and working with the incredible artists and designers at Epic made for an amazing time.

That need for new career experiences and new challenges comes at the cost of making me move onto new projects more often than others. That being said, I'm definitely a shipping kind of person. I know how to stay with a thing to get it out the door and beyond, but I definitely didn't stick around for Gears 2, 3, 4, or 5. I needed new challenges and ventured out to find them. I have mad respect for some of my fellow artists and ADs who have stuck it out at companies, on projects, with franchises for decades, but my path just doesn't flow that way.

Q. **What about the role is the most enjoyable to you? The part that gets you out of bed and keeps you motivated, that keeps the brain fizzing and sparking with creative ideas?**

A. Creating exciting experiences for players. I don't actually care if it's interactive, passive, live, recorded, I just want the thing I'm working on to have elements that are so unexpected you have to see it again. This is what drives me.

Sure, I have to work on things that fall into a much more traditional box, but it's the projects that push me and the team that get me out of bed. If it's scary and we're not sure we can pull it off, that's the project for me. I love working on the cutting edge. It requires outside-the-box problem solving all the time. It requires that each asset, each choice, each macro and micro decision are a mix of experience and guessing you've got it right. Adjusting constantly to things not working right, to things breaking, to the team being stretched beyond their inherent knowledge base.

The cutting edge is not for the faint of heart. I've worked on multi-million-dollar activations that ended badly because things failed at the worst possible times.

However, the rewards when you pull off something new is magical. It's the kind of feeling you only get a handful of times in a long career. I've been lucky enough to work with companies and teams who trust me enough to travel that path with me, to trust me that I can lead a team to something truly great.

Q. What's your least favourite part of the role? Anything common you've found from company to company, or does it depend on the environment? (There's no judgement here!)

A. My least favourite part of the role is likely the management side of things. Having spent a bunch of years directing, in a more traditional sense of the word, the video games industry's requirement that ADs are also managers is less than ideal.

Managing people and being able to lead a team of artists to make a cohesive visual statement are two completely different skills. The day-to-day role of art directing is communicating an artistic vision to a team and drive towards that vision across all the crafts. ADs work with design to understand the goals of the project so that the aesthetic choices complement and elevate the game's design and playstyle. This means the AD's job is to work with each of the visual crafts to create that cohesive visual wrapper for the core design and playstyle. From concept art to modelling to animation, each choice being made can